EZEKIEL

MESSAGES OF DISCIPLINE
AND LOVE

Ezekiel

Messages of Discipline and Love

F. Wayne Mac Leod

Authentic
MEDIA

© 2003 by F. Wayne Mac Leod

00 09 08 07 06 05 04   7 6 5 4 3 2 1
Authentic Lifestyle is an imprint of Authentic Media
PO Box 1047, 129 Mobilization Dr.
Waynesboro, GA 30830 USA
(706) 554-1594
authenticusa@stl.org

ISBN: 1-884543-92-8

Cover design: Paul Lewis

Contents

Preface

Why do I call this book a devotional commentary? While it is a commentary on the book of Ezekiel, its main objective is not to be scholarly or intellectual. It has as its purpose to help the reader see the practical application of the book to his or her own personal walk with God. I have tried my best to write this commentary on a level any reader can understand. This book is not meant to replace the Bible. Use this commentary in your quiet time with the Lord. Read the biblical passage along with the commentary. Take a moment to consider the questions at the end of each chapter. Conclude your time by praying about the things you have learned. I have also included some suggested prayer requests at the end of each chapter. Take a moment to pray over these requests.

Though written many hundreds of years ago, Ezekiel's prophecy is a modern commentary on our own society. It is my prayer that his voice will be heard again through this book. May God bless you as you take the time to hear what God has to teach you through his prophet Ezekiel.

F. Wayne Mac Leod

1

A Vision of God

Read Ezekiel 1

The last place we expect to meet God is in the midst of our trials. It seems that at these moments the Lord is distant. We wonder if he really is in control of our situation. The prophet Ezekiel began his ministry while the people of God were in their most difficult trial. They were in exile. It was here, however, that Ezekiel met the Lord God.

It all began at the Kebar River in Babylon. Here, by this river, the Spirit of the Lord came upon Ezekiel the priest. He saw a vision. In his vision a windstorm approached out of the north. To all appearances this storm was quite violent. A great cloud appeared. This cloud was engulfed in raging fire. There was a certain radiance about the cloud. The whole scene was surrounded by brilliant light coming from the cloud and fire. In the midst of that fire, Ezekiel saw four living creatures.

These creatures were strange in appearance. They had the general form of a man. Each of them, however, had four faces. Their four faces resembled a man, an ox, a lion, and an eagle (verse 10). They represented the greatest of God's creation. Man was the king of creation and was known for his intelligence. The ox was the king of the domesticated animals and was known for his hard work and strength. The lion was the king of the wild animals and was also known for his strength and speed. Finally, the eagle was the king of the birds, and it too was known for its speed and strength. Each of these four creatures had straight legs with feet like those of a calf. They sparkled with the color of bronze.

Each creature had four wings. Two of the wings covered its body, and two wings spread upward, touching the wings of the creatures next to it (verse 11). In order for this to happen, the creatures would have had to form either a box or a circle. The image here of the creatures touching each other's wings reminds us of the cherubim on the ark of the covenant whose wings touched above the cover of the ark. It was from between the wings of these cherubim that God gave his commands to his people (Exodus 25:22).

In Ezekiel's prophecy, fire moved among these creatures. Lightning flashed in their midst. They were awesome and powerful creatures. It is important that we note here that while this fire moved and flashed among these four creatures, it did not come from them. While they dwelt in the midst of this glory, the fire appears to have come from another source.

The scene before us reminds us of the vision of John in the book of Revelation. In Revelation 4 John saw four creatures around the throne of God that were very similar to these creatures seen here in Ezekiel. The creatures in Revelation 4, however, had only one face. Could John have seen the same creatures as the prophet Ezekiel?

As Ezekiel contemplated the scene before him, he noticed a wheel beside each of the creatures. The Bible tells us that Ezekiel was awestruck by these wheels. There were four wheels in all. Each wheel "appeared to be made like a wheel intersecting a wheel" (verse 16). They were made so they could roll in any direction (north, south, east, or west). The rims of the wheels were full of eyes (verse 18). The creatures of Revelation 4:6 were also filled with eyes. These wheels took the living creatures wherever they went (verses 19–21). Some commentators see here some sort of chariot. Ezekiel 1:21 tells us that the "spirit of the living creatures was in the wheels." Because each of the living creatures had four faces, they always moved straight ahead. Wherever the wheels went, the four living creatures were always prepared to follow. The sense here is that these four creatures were completely surrendered to the will of the wheels. They were not their own. God's will was their will.

Spread out above the living creatures was an expanse, as clear as sparkling ice or crystal (verse 22). A voice came from that expanse (verse 25). When Ezekiel looked up toward the source of the voice, he saw a great throne (verse 26). Above the throne was the form of a man. This man glowed like fire. Bright light surrounded him (verse 27). Here was the source of the fire and lightning. His appearance was like the glory of the Lord (verse 28). John's vision in Revelation 1:13–16 is very similar:

> and among the lampstands was someone "like a son of man," dressed in a robe reaching down to his feet and with a golden sash around his chest. His head and hair were white like wool, as white as snow, and his *eyes were like blazing fire. His feet were like bronze glowing in a furnace*, and his voice was like the sound of rushing waters. In his right hand he held seven stars, and out of his mouth came a sharp double-edged sword. His face was like the sun shining in all its brilliance. (emphasis mine)

While there is no question that Ezekiel was overwhelmed at the sight of the four living creatures, what he saw above the throne that day was far greater. Like the apostle John, Ezekiel fell to his face before the presence of this being. He was seeing God in all his glory.

Another important feature of this vision was the rainbow that Ezekiel saw (verse 28). The apostle John also saw a rainbow around the throne of God in heaven. The rainbow in the Old Testament reminds us of the covenant God made with Noah. Though he could have destroyed the earth by the flood, he chose to exercise grace and compassion. This rainbow represents the patience of a gracious and loving God. It is contrasted with the fire and lightning that came from the person on the throne. While he is a holy and awesome God, he is also a God who delights in showing mercy and compassion.

What does all this mean? Some commentators go to great lengths to discover the hidden meaning behind every aspect of this vision. This often leads to speculation. What we see before us is the very presence of the God of Israel revealed to Ezekiel. Angelic servants surrounded this awesome God. He was sovereign and almighty, yet gracious and loving. This was Ezekiel's God. This was the God he met in exile.

Ezekiel had caught a glimpse of the one and only true God of Israel. He saw the glory of God in the midst of his exile. His vision reminded him that God was still on the throne of the universe. The all-powerful and all-knowing God still reigned. There was reason to rejoice even in his exile.

God has not changed. What is your trial today? God is bigger than your trial. This sovereign God is working out his purposes for your life. He has not abandoned you. You can trust him fully. In Ezekiel's most difficult trial, he needed to see afresh that his God was a holy, all-powerful, and sovereign God. He needed to know that God had not abandoned his people. Maybe you too need to lift up your eyes and catch a glimpse of the great and awesome God we serve. To see him as he is will certainly change how we see our trials.

For Consideration:

- How would your attitude toward your present trials change if you could see, like Ezekiel, a holy and all-powerful God seated on his throne? Is God still on his throne today? How should this affect how you see your trial?

- What does this chapter reveal to you about God?

- Why is it so easy to lose sight of God in our pain? What causes us to lose sight of him?

For Prayer:

- Ask God to forgive you for the times you have forgotten that he is a holy and sovereign God.

- Ask him to enable you to place your confidence in him in your trial today.

- Thank him that no matter what happens, he is still in control.

2

Ezekiel's Call

Read Ezekiel 2:1–3:15

There are times in ministry when God's servants become discouraged. We sometimes wonder if anyone listens to what we say. We fail to see lives being touched as a result of our dedicated service. It is not easy to persevere in this situation. God knew that Ezekiel was no different from any other servant. He let the prophet know that his calling would be difficult. His success in that calling would be measured not by how many people listened to his message but, rather, by whether Ezekiel had been faithful in proclaiming his word.

In the last chapter we examined Ezekiel's vision of God. The God of Israel was so awesome that the prophet fell on his face before him. As he lay there a voice called out to him: "Stand on your feet and I will speak to you" (verse 1). Notice in verse 2 that it was not until the Spirit of God entered Ezekiel that he was able to rise to his feet. The impression we get here is that he was physically incapable of standing up without the strength the Spirit gave to him. Even as a prophet in Old

Testament times, this man had a very definite understanding of God and the work of his Spirit in his life.

When Ezekiel was set upon his feet, the Lord spoke to him. He told him that he was sending him to prophesy to a very rebellious people. They had sinned against the Lord for generations (verse 3). They were stubborn and impudent children (verse 4). God told Ezekiel in verse 5 that it was not important that he see results in his ministry. He was to proclaim the Word of God whether people listened or not. How often we get caught up in results. We measure the success or failure of a given ministry by its size and visible results. God told Ezekiel that he was not going to see these results. This was not God's purpose for Ezekiel. It is relatively easy to be faithful when things are going well and we are seeing all kinds of results in ministry. Ezekiel would have to be faithful even when people refused to listen. That was much harder.

God warned Ezekiel that when he walked among the people to whom he was sending him, it would be like walking among scorpions and thorns (verse 6). As he walked among them, they would sting him like scorpions. As he moved to avoid a scorpion, he would run into briers. These people would not appreciate him. They would make his life miserable. They were rebellious (verse 6) and hardhearted (3:7) and they would not listen to him (3:7). God warned the prophet that they would verbally attack him (verse 6). Ezekiel was not to be afraid of them or their words. Though they would not appreciate his presence among them, he was not to be dismayed (verse 6). The God who called him would also protect him.

We may wonder if it was worth going to this type of people. God made it clear to Ezekiel that this was indeed his will (verse 3). He was to tell them everything the Lord had given him (verses 4, 7). Whether the people listened or not, he was to be a faithful transmitter of the Word of God. Though they attacked him, Ezekiel was to persevere. Nothing was to stop him from proclaiming the Word of the Lord. We have to admire a man who would move out in obedience to the call of God under these conditions. God did not promise large followings. He did not promise success in the way the world sees it. Would you be willing to obey under these conditions? As Ezekiel considered the nature of his ministry, the Lord gave him a scroll (verse 10). Ezekiel noticed that it was filled with words of lament, mourning, and woe. The Lord told Ezekiel that he was to take this scroll and eat it. The apostle John was also asked to take a scroll and eat it (see Revelation 10:9–10). The idea here is that he was to digest the words in the scroll. He was to fill himself with its message and make it part of his very being. As Ezekiel ate the scroll he discovered that it was both bitter and sweet. This may represent both the curses and the blessings of the Word of God. The picture before us is a challenge for all ministers of the gospel. The Word of God is to be our constant food. We are to daily digest it until it becomes part of our very being. How can we preach to others when what we preach has not become part of us?

In Ezekiel 3:4 the Lord reminded the prophet that he was sending him to the house of Israel. He was not called to be a missionary like the prophet Jonah. Ezekiel's ministry would be among his own people. Verse 5 tells us that he was not being sent to a people who spoke in an unfamiliar tongue or language that was hard to learn. His ministry would have been much easier had he been called to foreign missions. These people would have listened to him. His own people, however, were hardened to the Word of God. They would have nothing to do with his message. Very often those who have never heard the gospel are more willing to receive it than those who have heard it for years.

Though the people Ezekiel was being called to were hard, God promised to make Ezekiel even harder: "But I will make you as unyielding and hardened as they are. I will make your forehead like the hardest stone, harder than flint. Do not be afraid of them or terrified by them, though they are a rebellious house" (verses 8–9). God would give him the strength necessary for this difficult task. What is God calling you to do? You can be sure that no matter how difficult that task may be, he who calls you will strengthen you for the task if you let him.

Notice in verse 10 that Ezekiel was to receive the Word of God *in his heart*. Having done so, he would then be able to preach with passion. His preaching would come from his heart and not just his mind. The most powerful sermons I have ever heard have come from the heart of God's servants. This is what God expected of Ezekiel. As a prophet he was to have a prophet's heart—a heart that was broken by those things that broke the heart of God. All too often we preach intellectual sermons. God is not looking for people who have knowledge of the truth so much as people who are truly touched by that truth in the very core of their being. He calls us to preach and share from hearts that are in touch with him and share his passion and burden.

After these things the Spirit of God moved Ezekiel to the river where he had received his calling (see chapter 1). Notice in verse 14 that he went in "bitterness" and "in the heat of his spirit" (NKJV). What was causing this bitterness? Was it the ministry that God was calling him to? It was, indeed, a very difficult ministry. Was he bitter toward God for giving him such a hard ministry? While this is possible, there is another possibility we need to consider. Could it be that the bitterness was caused by the work of the Spirit of God in his life? God's Spirit had fallen upon Ezekiel. He saw things in a different light now that he had this vital encounter with God. His heart was now in tune with the heart of God. The things that grieved the heart of God now grieved him. Part of the equipping of Ezekiel was that God needed to give him eyes that saw what God saw. He needed to have a heart that felt what God felt. The role of the Spirit of God here was to cause him to see the world as God saw it. This was in reality the prophetic gift.

His heart was heavy because of the sin of God's people. Only when he had experienced this burden could he truly preach as God expected him to preach. Only when his heart was broken could he preach with the passion God required from him. The role of prophet was a difficult one. It was far more than speaking words. It was sharing the heart of God. Do you have the heart of God? Is your heart burdened with the things that burden God's heart? This was all part of the preparation of Ezekiel for the prophetic ministry God had in store for him.

The Spirit of God led Ezekiel to Tel Abib. This would be the starting point of his ministry. Verse 15 tells us that for seven days Ezekiel remained in the city and felt overwhelmed. What he had experienced in his calling was so powerful that for a whole week he could do nothing but marvel at what he had seen and heard. You can be sure that he thought a lot about what had taken place the last few days. His experience of God was not one he would soon forget. It would change his life and powerfully impact his ministry. This is where all ministries should start—with a deep and powerful encounter with God. It was this personal knowledge of God and God's will for his life that would take him through the times of rejection and persecution he was going to face.

What does all this have to do with us today? You may not always understand the ways of the Lord. You do not need to understand—just be obedient. It is true that the path is not always easy. We will be called upon to endure many hardships. Even our Lord was rejected. We cannot expect to be treated any better. Be assured, however, that God's strength is equal to the task. When the situation gets hard, God will make you harder. He will never give you a task to do without giving you the strength necessary to accomplish that task. He will never cause you to face a trial that he has not equipped you to face. He will never cause you to be tempted beyond your ability to resist. The sovereign God of chapter 1 would stand beside Ezekiel in his ministry. Ezekiel would know his strength and enabling. That same God stands by you and me today. In his strength we are more than overcomers.

For Consideration:

- Why is it so tempting to get caught up in the idea that success equals large followings? How does what Ezekiel learned here teach us that this is wrong?

- What is success in ministry according to what we learn here in this section?

- What promises does God give to those who are willing to step out in obedience?

- What are the qualifications required here for a servant of God who ministers in his name?

For Prayer:

- Ask God to give you the boldness of Ezekiel to step out unhindered by what others may say or think.

- Ask God to give you his mind so that you would see people as he sees them.

- One of the key requirements of being a servant is to personally have an encounter with God. Ask God to reveal himself in a deeper way to you today.

3

The Watchman

Read Ezekiel 3:16–27

D id you ever have a job as a watchman or a guard? We should not underestimate the importance of this job. In the days of Ezekiel these individuals held the lives of the nation in their hands. The success or failure of an army often depended on the alertness of their watchmen. Ezekiel was to be a watchman for the people of God. As a watchman he had the responsibility of warning the people of coming danger. This was not a task to be taken lightly. The life of his people depended on him. He needed to be alert.

As a watchman, Ezekiel had responsibility toward two groups of people: the wicked and the righteous. In verse 18 we see that Ezekiel was to warn the wicked of coming judgment. If God told him that the wicked would die and he did not warn them of their approaching judgment, God would require their blood "at his hands" (NKJV). He would be held responsible for their death. If he warned them and they refused to listen, they would die but Ezekiel would be free of their blood. As a watchman, Ezekiel's task was not to convince people—it was to warn them. The measure of his success was not counted in responses to his message but, rather, in his obedience to proclaim the truth and warn the people. In an age that measures success in numbers, we need to hear what God is saying here.

The righteous also needed to be warned (see verses 20–21). Even the people of God are tempted to turn their eyes away for him for a moment. David committed adultery. Peter denied knowing the Lord. As a prophet of God Ezekiel was to exhort and warn his own brothers and sisters when they fell away. If he refused to warn a brother when the Lord told him to do so, Ezekiel would be held accountable.

Verse 20 tells us that God places a "stumbling block" in front of the righteous who sin. Our sin will sometimes lead to a withdrawal of God's blessing. Paul speaks of believers becoming sick and even dying because of their persistence in sin (see 1 Corinthians 11:30). We have a definite responsibility toward our brothers and sisters in the Lord. We are called to warn those who wander from the path of righteousness. We dare not stand on the sidelines watching our brother fall into sin without calling out to him and warning him of the dangers that lie ahead. While he may not listen to us, we owe it to him to warn him of the danger of persisting in his ways. God expected Ezekiel to watch for signs of the enemy's presence. He was to warn his own brothers and sisters of the presence of the enemy.

All of this meant that the prophet needed to be very much in tune with the Lord. He had to be listening to what the Lord was telling him. His relationship with God had to be intimate. Like a watchman, he needed to be spiritually alert to God's Word and the situation around him. His ears needed to be constantly listening for the Word of the Lord. He needed to be ready at the slightest indication to warn those who needed to be warned.

In verses 22–23 the Lord called Ezekiel to go to a plain where he spoke to him. Here he came face to face with the glory of the God he had seen at the Kebar River. Once again, the prophet was overwhelmed by what he saw. He fell on his face before the Lord. Again, it is only when the Spirit of God came upon him that he was able to get back on his feet (see verse 24). For the previous few weeks, Ezekiel had been on a spiritual high. He had seen visions of God that had literally thrown him to the ground in awe. He had been commissioned and empowered for a very particular ministry on God's behalf. These were days he would not soon forget.

God reminded Ezekiel here that the people to whom he would prophesy would not appreciate him. They would tie him down with ropes so that he could not circulate among them preaching the Word of God (verses 24–25). God himself would make his tongue stick to the roof of his mouth so that he would not be able to speak to these people. Why did God do this? He did it because these people were a rebellious people. They were not ready to listen to the Word of God. They would die in their sin for their rebellion. They would not be given another chance to repent. God alone knows when you have heard the last call. There would come a time when God would no longer speak to these people. He would withdraw from them, and they would perish in their sin. How dangerous it is to keep putting off God in our lives!

We see from verse 26 that sometimes God would make Ezekiel's tongue stick to the roof of his mouth. In verse 27 we discover that there would be other times when the Lord would expect him to speak out. Not only was Ezekiel to be sensitive to what the Lord wanted him to communicate, he also needed to know when the Lord wanted him to speak and when he needed to be silent. This required being very much in tune with the Lord God and his will. Is your relationship with the Lord such that he could lead you to certain individuals with a specific word of warning or encouragement? Would you be able to discern his leading when he told you not to speak? It is physically impossible for us to reach everyone. This passage does not call us to leave our jobs and responsibilities to go out with the gospel to every person we meet. It does challenge us, however, to be so in tune with the Lord God and his leading in our lives that whenever he has a word of exhortation, warning, or encouragement for a brother or sister, we will hear his voice and respond in obedience.

Ezekiel's call could not be taken lightly. People's lives depended on his warnings. He needed to be spiritually alert. We need men and women like this today. What a challenge these verses are to us! Do you have on your hands the blood of men and women you should have warned? I am not saying that you need to give up everything and speak to every person you meet. I am saying, however, that we all need to learn to listen to the Lord and follow his leading. God will not hold you responsible for those to whom he has not called you to go. He will hold you accountable for those to whom he has personally called you to minister. Are you willing to follow God's leading at any moment? Are you a watchman? May you be a faithful watchman.

For Consideration:

- What does it mean to be a watchman?

- Are there things we need to be warning our neighbors about? How about our brothers and sisters in Christ? Be specific.

- Have you ever experienced the clear leading of God to speak to a certain individual? Explain.

For Prayer:

- Ask God to make you sensitive to his leading in your life.

- Ask him to forgive you for the times you have failed to speak to those to whom he has called you to speak.

- As his servant, ask him for boldness to be obedient to his prompting

4

Baked Bread and Cow Dung

Read Ezekiel 4

L ike many other prophets, Ezekiel was encouraged to use visual object lessons. These object lessons presented the Word of God to the people in a way they could understand. In this passage Ezekiel was to act out, in a dramatic way, the message God had for his people.

First, God asked the prophet to draw a picture of the city of Jerusalem on a clay tablet. This would serve as a prop for the message the prophet was to communicate to his people. Ezekiel was then to make a small ramp and battering ram and set them up around the city drawn on the tablet. All around this city there was to be a visual representation of the enemy camp.

Having set up these props, he was then to take an iron pan and place it between him and the city, like a wall. Having done so, he was then to turn his face away from the city. What is the meaning of this scene? Very clearly, the city drawn on the tablet represented the city of Jerusalem which would be besieged by the enemy. The iron pan seems to represent the sins of the people, which had put a barrier between them and their God so that he had to turn his face from them in their time of need. The scene before us was simple enough for a child to understand.

With the visual representation of the city under siege before him, the prophet was then to lie on his side and symbolically bear the sins of the people. Each day that he lay on his side represented a year that the nation had turned her back on the Lord God. Three hundred and ninety days were assigned to Ezekiel for the land of Israel. Forty days were assigned to the nation of Judah. Ezekiel 4:8 tells us that the Lord would tie the prophet with cords so that he could not move during this time. It is unclear how this would take place.

We have to admire Ezekiel. It is relatively easy to be faithful in big things. God asked him here, however, to lay on his side for over a year. This was to be his ministry. It was not a spectacular ministry. There may have been times when he wondered if there weren't something better for him. It is not easy to be laid up on a bed of sickness or to have to wait patiently upon the Lord for his timing in a matter. God expected obedience from Ezekiel, no matter what the cost. We like to be busy. God calls us to be obedient. We may not understand God's methods, but his ways are perfect. We have a tendency to rush ahead and seek the big and flashy ministries. Sometimes God simply calls us to lie on our side and wait upon him.

Three hundred and ninety days were assigned to the land of Israel (verses 4–5). There is much speculation about the number 390. During the reign of Rehoboam, in 931 B.C., the tribes of Israel separated from Judah, forming their own nation. Jereboam became the king of Israel, while Rehoboam reigned over Judah. Jereboam established a new religion and priesthood in Israel. From that time forward, Israel did not serve the Lord as a nation. One evil king after another reigned until the land was destroyed by the Assyrians, and the Israelites were taken into captivity. It was not until 538 B.C. (393 years after the division of Israel and Judah) that King Cyrus issued a decree to send the Jews back to their homeland. Could it be that the 390 years mentioned here is the time between the separation of Israel from Judah and the return from exile to rebuild? However we see this, what is clear is that God had patiently endured Israel's sin for 390 years!

When Ezekiel had finished the 390 days of lying on his left side for Israel, the Lord called him to lie on his right side for forty days more to proclaim the judgment against Judah. There are a couple of things we need to note here. It may be significant that Ezekiel lay on his right side for Judah. The right hand, or the right side, in Scripture represents favor. For example, when the Lord Jesus returned to his Father, he sat on his right hand. In other words, he took the place of honor. The other thing we need to see here is that the time given to Judah was not as long as that of Israel. While the northern nation of Israel lived in complete rebellion, Judah was different. She had kings who served the Lord. Judah experienced several spiritual revivals in her history. Unlike Jereboam, who set up his own priesthood, Judah continued to serve the Lord through the priesthood God had established.

God assigned 390 years of sin and rebellion to Israel but only forty years to Judah. Each day that Ezekiel lay on his side represented a year that God had to patiently bear the sins of his people. God was demonstrating very graphically how patient he had been toward them. The people of his day would have understood this. Imagine people passing by each day, seeing Ezekiel lying on his side. Each day they wondered how long he was going to stay there. They would be struck by Ezekiel's patience in this matter. This was the whole point of this illustration. It all pointed to how patient God had been with his people in their sin.

While this ministry in itself was a very difficult one, the matter complicated itself in Ezekiel 4:9–15. God told the prophet what he was to eat during this time. He was to eat eight ounces (200 grams) of bread each day at set times throughout the day. This amount of bread would be equivalent to one French bread stick per day. He could also have two-thirds of a quart of water a day (0.6 liters). For over a year the prophet was to remain on this diet of bread and water. As if this was not difficult enough, the Lord asked him to bake his bread over a fire made from dried human excrement. When Ezekiel protested, the Lord agreed to allow him to prepare his bread on a fire made from dried cow manure. What did this represent? It reminded the people of God that times would be difficult for them. Famine and poverty would certainly be their lot. Their bread would be rationed out, and the only firewood available to them would be their own dried excrement.

This chapter causes us to ask a very important question: Why was Ezekiel prophesying of the downfall of Jerusalem when he was already in exile? The exile of God's people came in various stages. According to Ezekiel 1:2 this prophecy came in the fifth year of the exile of Jehoiachin. After the exile of Jehoiachin, Zedekiah became king in Judah. At this point, though some had already been exiled, many people still remained in the land of Judah. The Bible tells us that Zedekiah reigned eleven years in the land (Jeremiah 52:1). It was during the reign of Zedekiah that Nebuchadnezzar took the city. He blocked all food supplies, causing this great famine of which Ezekiel was prophesying. In the eleventh year of Zedekiah (seven years after Ezekiel received his prophetic call), Nebuchadnezzar destroyed Jerusalem (see 2 Kings 25). Obviously, Ezekiel had been taken into exile many years before the destruction of Jerusalem and the final exodus of God's people.

What does all of this have to do with us? Does this

passage not show us the commitment of Ezekiel to obey the words of the Lord? Who among us would be willing to stay on a diet of bread and water for over a year to get a message across to the people of God? How many among us would be willing to submit to lying on our sides for the same period of time? To what lengths would you go to proclaim the Word of the Lord? Ezekiel is a challenge to those of us who have become comfortable in our lifestyle. Oh, that there were more men and women like Ezekiel who were willing to endure hardship for the sake of the Word of the Lord!

In an age when we are looking for big churches and large followings, God reveals to us the ministry of a faithful servant who persevered in the small and seemingly insignificant. He challenges us in our success-oriented society to learn to be faithful even in small things. May God forgive us for seeing ministry as a means of advancing our own reputations. May he give us more Ezekiels who care nothing for this world or their reputations—people whose desire is to step out in obedience, regardless of the cost.

For Consideration:

- Why do you suppose God wanted Ezekiel to act out his message rather than simply speak to the people?

- Place yourself in Ezekiel's shoes for a moment. How would you feel if God were to ask you to do what he asked Ezekiel to do? What would this have done to Ezekiel's reputation?

- How does this passage speak to our success-oriented society? How does this challenge us today?

- Have you ever had to wait upon the Lord? How difficult was it?

For Prayer:

- Ask God for the strength to obey even as Ezekiel obeyed.

- Ask God to set you free from self and pride so that you would obey, regardless of the cost.

5
A Condemned People

Read Ezekiel 5

We have seen that the ministry of the prophet Ezekiel was not an easy one. The people he worked with were described as scorpions. God had told him that they would not listen to his message. In the last chapter we saw how Ezekiel was called to lie on his side for more than a year to symbolize the sin of the people of God. During this time he lived on a diet of bread and water. There may have been times when he wondered if this was really what he wanted to do with his life. Things do not get any easier for the prophet. Here in chapter 5 God gave Ezekiel a message for his people.

Ezekiel's message to the people began with a symbolic act. After having completed his days of lying on his side, the Lord asked him to shave his head. In Bible times the act of shaving the head was a sign of mourning. People in Ezekiel's day, seeing this, would understand that something terrible was about to happen.

Verse 2 tells us that Ezekiel was to take his hair and divide it into three parts. One-third of the hair was to be burned in the midst of the city. The second third was to be struck with his sword. The final third was to be scattered to the wind. The Lord asked Ezekiel to keep a few strands safely in his garment (verse 3). Ezekiel was to later take a few of these strands of hair and cast them into the fire. We will see the significance of this in a moment.

The people would not have understood what Ezekiel was doing. God was showing his people what was about to happen to them. Jerusalem had rebelled against the laws of God. She had become worse than the pagans around her. She had refused the Word of God. There was now more corruption and sin in Israel than in the surrounding nations. As children of God, they had not been living up to God's standard. Because they had turned their backs on God, they would be punished. Listen to how God described their punishment: "Because of all your detestable idols, I will do to you what I have never done before and will never do again" (verse 9).

The punishment of God's people would be more severe than any nation before them had ever experienced. We understand the truth of this statement in our day in a way Ezekiel never understood it. We have seen the Jewish nation suffer more than any other nation. They have been in constant warfare. They have been oppressed and ridiculed throughout history. What a warning this is to us who claim to be Christians today. We cannot take our commitment to the Lord Jesus lightly.

God told Ezekiel about the coming judgment of his people. The famine in the land would be so great that fathers would be forced to eat their own children to survive. Children would eat their parents (verse 10). The nation would be scattered (verse 10). God would diminish them because they had defiled his sanctuary (verse 11). They had been blessed of God, but now he would no longer have any pity on them (verse 11). One-third of them would perish by the famine that would take place in the land (verse 12). One-third of them would fall by the sword of their enemy (verse 12). The final third would be scattered and pursued by their enemy at the point of the sword (verse 12). The whole nation would become a ruin (verse 14). They would be a reproach to the nations around them (verse 14). This is what Ezekiel was symbolizing with his shaved hair.

We have seen the significance of the dividing up of Ezekiel's hair. You will recall in verse 3, however, that there were a few strands that the prophet took and placed in the hem of his garment for safekeeping. Even these strands were to be taken out and burned (see verse 4). It appears that these strands of hair represented those who had been originally spared from the judgment of God in the form of fire, sword, and exile (scattering). There were those who remained in the land after the exile who still rebelled against the Lord. They did not learn their lesson. In the book of Jeremiah, we read how these individuals wanted to return to Egypt. God warned them through his prophet Jeremiah that they would perish in Egypt. Despite this warning, they returned to the land that God had delivered them from under Moses. It could be that these strands represented these individuals.

Verse 13 reminds us that God would be avenged because of the sin of his people. They would know that God was serious about sin. What took place in their midst would serve as a lesson to the nations (verse 15). God would execute his judgment against them in anger and fury (verse 15 NKJV). He would strike them with the arrow of famine. God would shoot to kill (verse 16). Those the famine did not devour, the wild beast would kill (verse 17). They would be "childless" (verse 17). Plagues and bloodshed would sweep the land (verse 17). The sword of God's wrath would come upon them (verse 17).

The Bible tells us that this punishment was to serve as an example for the nations. We are those nations. We need to take this lesson seriously. We cannot take our commitment to the Lord lightly. How is your relationship with the Lord today? Consider the message of the prophet Ezekiel to the people of God in his day. May their experience serve as a warning to us.

For Consideration:

• Is the Lord just in his punishment of his people here in this chapter? Explain.

• Consider for a moment that these people under judgment are the people of God. What do you suppose God would have to say to his people today? Can we compare Israel of Ezekiel's day to the contemporary church? Give some examples.

• What keeps God from exercising his judgment on our society today?

For Prayer:

• Take a moment to examine your own life. Are there things in your life that need to be dealt with? Ask God to forgive you and give you victory.

• Ask God to send a revival to cleanse and renew his people today.

• Thank God for his great patience with us.

6
Then You Will Know

Read Ezekiel 6

We do not always understand why God disciplines us as he does. We can be assured, however, that our discipline is never without cause. Through our discipline, God teaches us some very important lessons. He disciplines us for our good. His desire is to draw us closer to himself.

As we begin this chapter, the prophet Ezekiel was called upon to set his face against the mountains of Israel and prophesy against them. What took place on the mountains that caused God to send his prophet to prophesy against them? The mountains and the hills of Israel were where God's people had set up their altars to worship foreign gods. Both Isaiah and Jeremiah spoke of this evil practice among the people of God. In Jeremiah 3:6 the LORD asked, "Have you seen what faithless Israel has done? *She has gone up on every high hill* and under every spreading tree and has committed adultery there" (emphasis mine). In Isaiah 65:7 the LORD said, "Because *they burned sacrifices on the mountains and defied me on the hills,* I will measure into their laps the full payment for their former deeds" (emphasis mine).

The mountaintops and hilltops in Israel were the places where God's people played the harlot. It was here that they blasphemed the name of the Lord their God by worshiping other gods. For this reason the prophet was called upon to prophesy against the mountains and the hills of Israel. Notice in verse 3 that Ezekiel was also to prophesy against the valleys and the rivers of the land. In 2 Chronicles 28:3 we are told what took place in the valleys of Israel: "He burned sacrifices in the Valley of Ben Hinnom and sacrificed his sons in the fire, following the detestable ways of the nations the LORD had driven out before the Israelites." The most detestable of all the practices of the children of Israel took place in the valley. Here God's people practiced child sacrifice to the honor of the pagan gods.

God was angry with his people. They had filled both the mountaintops and the valleys with their spiritual prostitution. The whole land was saturated with the horrible practices of the nations. Israel had abandoned her God. She would not go unpunished.

Because they had turned their backs on God, Ezekiel prophesied that their places of worship would be destroyed. Their foreign altars would be demolished (verse 4). The bones of the worshipers would be scattered all around their altars (verse 5). Their dwelling places would be laid waste (verse 6). The bodies of the slain would be strewn across the land (verse 7). The scene before us is one of utter devastation. God did not take great delight in destroying the land. He was compelled by their disobedience, however, to judge. His desire was not to destroy them but to teach them a very important lesson: "Your people will fall slain among you, and you will know that I am the LORD" (verse 7).

It is important that we understand that the reason God

was disciplining his people was so that they could know him in a deeper way. His desire was to enter into a very deep and intimate relationship with his people. There had been many things that had separated him from them. God loved them enough to do something about it. He would remove those obstacles. When the obstacles were removed, then they would know him to be the one true Lord. The first thing God did in this chapter to restore fellowship with his people was to remove the obstacles that separated them from him. He took away their places of pagan worship.

After removing the obstacles, notice what God did in verses 8 and 9. Those whom God spared from disaster would remember God among the nations where they were scattered. There in the land of their exile, they would come under the convicting power of the Spirit of God. Ezekiel 6:9 tells us that they would know how much they had broken the heart of God because of their sins. They would loathe themselves because of their evil ways and practices.

Notice here in verse 9 that God is crushed by our rebellion. His heart is grieved when we wander from the truth into error. My sin affects God. His desire for communion is so great that he is saddened and even crushed because of my sin. To enable his people to return to him, God had broken them physically. Now here, he broke them spiritually. Before restoration comes brokenness. We need to see our sin before we can truly return to God.

God would strike the land. People would die because of their detestable practices. They would fall by the sword, by famine, and by plague (verse 11). Their evil practices had angered God. To show them how angry he was with their sin, God told the prophet Ezekiel to pound his fists and stamp his feet before the people while shouting out, "Alas!" Why was God so angry? He was angry because his people had treated their relationship with him so lightly. He was angry because they preferred their foreign gods to him. He is a jealous God. He cries out for our attention and love. This is something we may never fully understand. Why would the great Creator God so love me? While we may never be able to explain it, we dare not refuse such a wonderful love.

God's wrath would be poured out on his rebellious people. The bodies of the slain would be scattered around their foreign altars, on the mountaintops, and under the shade trees throughout the land. In that day they would know that the Lord was God. Verse 14 tells us that the whole land would be desolate. From the northern city of Diblah to the most southern city, the whole land would be wasted. Wherever the people lived, they would live in desolation.

While the discipline of God was very harsh, it was not without its purpose. God was trying to get the attention of his people. They would not listen to his prophets. They would not learn from the experience of their forefathers. God was forced to remove the obstacles that kept his people from listening to him. He destroyed their land because it was not as important to him as his relationship with his people. He took them from their homes and took their freedom from them because it stood in the way of their communion with God. Anything that stood between them and God was removed. His love for them was so great that he was willing to take everything from them if, by so doing, intimacy could be restored. What keeps you from God? What would God have to remove from your life to get your full attention? God's people needed to be brought to a point of absolute brokenness before they would listen to him. The removal of their blessings was a blessing in itself. Through their brokenness, they were brought to a place of greater intimacy with God.

For Consideration:

- What stands between you and greater intimacy with God today?

- What are some of the obstacles to faith in God in our society and church today?

- What would it take for God to remove these obstacles?

- What would you be willing to give up in order to experience greater intimacy with God?

- What do we learn here about the love of the Lord for his people?

For Prayer:

- Has anything come between you and God? What are these things? Ask God to forgive you for allowing them to come between you and him.

- Ask him to remove those things in your life that hinder your spiritual growth and maturity. If you can't ask him for this, then ask him to make you willing.

- Are you facing his discipline now? Thank him that his discipline is for your good.

7

The End Is Come

Read Ezekiel 7

Have you ever had something tragic happen to you? Tragedy is one of those things that is supposed to happen to someone else. It is not supposed to happen to me. Tragedy always takes us by surprise.

God told his people here that their end had come. This end did not come suddenly. They had every opportunity to turn to the Lord, but they refused. Now they would pay the price. In verse 2 the Lord told them that the end had come upon the four corners of the land. In other words, the whole land would suffer the consequences of sin.

Verse 3 reminds us that the judgment of the Lord was righteous. They would only be judged according to their ways. What they received now from the hand of the Lord was only a repayment for what they had done to him. Consider this thought for a moment: What would you receive from the Lord if he gave you what you deserved? God told his people here that he would give them what they deserved. This ought to strike terror into our own hearts, for we have all fallen short of the standard that God has set for us. Praise God for his grace toward us. Because of Christ, our sins have been forgiven and cleansed. The wonderful news of the gospel is that we do not get what we deserve. Let's be careful, however, so that we don't turn our backs on the Lord Jesus and his mercy and place ourselves in the same situation as the people of Israel in this passage.

The wrath of God was very real. Because his people had persisted in their rebellion against him, God would show no pity. They would not be spared. Their end had come. On that day, God's fury and anger would be poured out (verse 8). The day of accounting and judgment was coming. What horrible words these are. One day these words will again be repeated. Today is a day of grace. Today God is extending his hand to you to offer you mercy and pardon. If you refuse that pardon and grace today, you will one day hear him say, "Your end has come." The day is coming when the last call will be issued and the train will pull out of the station and you will be left behind to face the wrath and fury of a God who pleaded with you all your life.

When will that day come for you and me? None of us knows. For these people, the day had come. For you and me, it could be any time. How quickly life can be cut off! None of us knows from one day to another if we will be able to make it through the day. I remember preaching in a downtown mission to street people in Toronto. After preaching the gospel, a man came forward to speak to me about the Lord. We spoke for some time, and I asked him if he had ever accepted the Lord Jesus into his heart. He said he hadn't. I asked him if he wanted to seek his forgiveness right then. He said, "I think I'll wait until I get home" (wherever that was). I reminded him that he really didn't even know if he was going to get home that night. I don't know if he ever opened his heart to the Lord. I never saw him after that meeting. We have no guarantee of tomorrow.

Ezekiel used the symbol of a budding rod in verse 10. This illustration takes us back to the days when the people of God complained about Aaron being the leader. God gave them a sign. Each of them brought a rod and placed it before the Lord. The rod that budded would be a sign from the Lord that the person who owned the rod was his chosen servant. Aaron's rod not only budded but produced blossoms and fruit. This was a sign from the Lord. God reminded his people here that there would also be signs of his judgment of sin. Israel's rods had budded and produced fruit of wickedness. Now they would pay the price for their evil.

No one would escape this judgment (verse 11). No one would mourn for them in their day of judgment. Both the buyer and the seller would grieve. The buyer would grieve because he would not enjoy what he had purchased. The seller would grieve because he would not be able to enjoy the profits from his sales. His life would be cut short. Nothing of what they had accumulated in this life would help them in the day of accounting. All they had would be taken from them. They would be left barren. They had not invested in spiritual matters, and now they would be left with nothing.

The trumpet would be blown and people would be made ready, but no one would go to battle. They would be struck even before they would have an opportunity to fight. They would perish by sword, famine, and pestilence. Those who survived would be scattered (see verse 16). Ezekiel had symbolized this day in chapter 5 when he shaved his head and divided up his hair into three piles (see Ezekiel 5:1–4, 12). That day of judgment would be a day of great shame and humiliation.

Their money would not rescue them from the wrath of God. Their silver and gold would no longer amount to power. They would not be able to bribe God with their wealth. They would not be able to hire anyone who could protect them from the wrath of God. On the day of God's wrath, their abundance would not even buy them the immediate essentials of life. They would throw their silver and their gold into the streets like "an unclean thing" (verse 19). There would be nothing to buy because all their blessings would be handed over to the nations as plunder (verses 20–21).

The enemy would invade their land and take their possessions. God would not stop them from profaning the temple. There was no place the enemy would not go (verse 22). God's people would be left wondering if God was in all this. They had not honored him in the temple, and so God would take it from them. The Gentiles would come in and take over both the land and the temple. We need to ask ourselves if this has not already happened in many cases in our land and church today. There are whole churches today filled with unbelievers. There are pastors ministering from the pulpits of our land who know nothing about what it means to accept the Lord Jesus as their Savior and Lord. Sunday School classes are being taught by teachers who have never repented of their sins. Has the temple of our day been given over to foreigners, even as it was in the days of Ezekiel?

In their sin and rebellion, God's people would be unable to find the peace they sought. Without God, their hearts would be empty. They would call upon the prophets, but the prophets would have no visions. The Lord would be silent (verse 26). When they turned to their priests, they would discover that the teaching of the law was lost. Even their priests would not have an answer for them. The elders of the land would have no counsel to give them. When their religious leaders could not help them, they would turn to their political leaders. Their king, however, would be found in mourning and the princes, in desolation (verse 27). There would be no help found in their political leaders. Their attention would turn to the other "people of the land." Everyone, however, would be as troubled as they were and would offer no solution to their problem (verse 27).

This truly would be the end. There would be absolutely nothing that they could do to protect themselves. They had exhausted every possibility. There would be no one who could come to their rescue. They were destined for the wrath of God.

Ezekiel is warning us of the dangers of living our lives in rebellion against God. The day of the wrath of God is coming. There is a time when the Lord Jesus will return to judge the world. On that day, your money will amount to nothing. You will not be able to sit down and negotiate your punishment with the Lord. Your friends, religious leaders, or political leaders will not be able to help you. You will stand alone before your judge. You will answer to him alone and receive your sentence. The time is coming when God will judge. He will not always strive with us. This chapter is a real warning for us. We need to examine our lives to be sure that we are right with God. For the moment, he extends his pardon and compassion to us. The day is coming, however, when he will withdraw his offer of pardon and give us what we deserve. Today is the day of salvation. Today is the day of repentance. Don't let another moment pass without surrendering to the will of the Lord.

For Consideration:

- Consider for a moment the evidences of God's grace in your life. Are there times when he did not give you what you deserved?

- If God does not presently give us what we deserve, why do we still need to concern ourselves with living for him? Why can't we simply live the way we want?

- Is there evidence of the "temple being given over to foreigners" today? Give some practical examples of this.

- In their day of judgment, the people came to the priests and prophets for help but found none. If these people came to you or your church personally, would they find the help they needed?

For Prayer:

- Are there things in your life that need to be confessed? Take a moment to confess these sins to God.

- Ask God to cleanse his church today. Pray for those churches that are being led by leaders who do not personally know the Lord.

- Ask God to cleanse you and make you ready for his return.

8

A Vision of
the Temple

Read Ezekiel 8

As Ezekiel was sitting in his house with the elders of the land, the Spirit of the Lord came upon him. We are not told why the elders had come to Ezekiel's house. Had they come of their own free will to hear the Word of the Lord, or had they been compelled to come? We are not sure. What is clear is that while the elders were with Ezekiel, the hand of the Lord came upon him in their presence. We have the impression here that the prophet waited for God to speak. God came upon him in his own time. In our modern day with our busy schedules, we no longer seem to have the time to wait for God.

In the presence of the elders, the prophet was taken up in a vision. Ezekiel saw the figure of someone who looked like a man. This individual, however, from the waist down, was full of fire. From the waist up, he glowed like amber. This description should be familiar to us. This is the same person that Ezekiel saw in chapter 1 (see Ezekiel 1:26–27). When the prophet saw him on that first occasion, he fell down on his face and worshiped him. There can be little doubt but that it is the Lord Jesus Christ in his glory that Ezekiel saw here.

As Ezekiel watched, this individual stretched out his hand, picked him up by the hair, and brought him to a place he described as being somewhere between heaven and earth. In his vision the prophet was brought to the city of Jerusalem. He stood at the north gate of the temple's inner court. As Ezekiel looked around, he noticed an idol. We have no description of the idol. It should not have been there in the temple. It is described as being an idol that "provokes to jealousy" (verse 3). God is not a God who will share his glory with another. This idol had provoked him to jealousy.

In stark contrast to this terrible idol discovered in the temple, Ezekiel had a real deep sense of the presence of the Lord in that place. He reminds us that the glory he experienced that day in the vision was like the experience he described for us in the beginning of his book. He was aware of the presence of the same God who called him into his prophetic ministry. It is hard to imagine what this contrast did for Ezekiel. On the one hand, he knew the powerful presence of a holy God who inspires fear. On the other hand, he saw the wickedness of people as they blasphemed the name of this great and holy God in the very temple where he was to be worshiped. Ezekiel was caught between these two extremes.

As he waited, Ezekiel heard the voice of the Lord: "Do you see what they are doing—the utterly detestable things the house of Israel is doing here, things that will drive me far from my sanctuary?" (verse 6). God reminded Ezekiel that these practices would drive his presence away from his people. God took this matter very seriously. He would not remain in a place where he was being blasphemed. He would withdraw his presence and his blessing if this practice continued. What a powerful warning this is for us in our day! Imagine what your society would be like if the Lord God withdrew his presence. Imagine what your church would be like if God withdrew his blessing.

Ezekiel was then led to the door of the temple court where he discovered a hole in the wall. The Lord told the prophet to dig out this hole. After digging through the hole in the wall, Ezekiel noticed a doorway. He was commanded to go through the door. Ezekiel entered, and there before him, portrayed on the walls, were all sorts of detestable animals and idols. These animals and creeping things were unclean and abominable in the eyes of the Lord. According to the law of God, the Israelites were not even to touch these animals, so they would not be defiled. Ezekiel saw these unclean objects, however, in the temple of God. To add to this, Ezekiel counted seventy elders, with censors in hand, offering incense to these abominable images. Were these the elders who sat before him in his house? Was God revealing to Ezekiel the secret practices of the elders who sat before him? How would they respond to this vision?

"Have you seen what the elders of the house of Israel are doing in the darkness?" God asked Ezekiel (verse 12). They believed that the Lord did not see what they were doing in secret. God reminded them, however, that he saw everything they did. I can just see the elders in Ezekiel's house that day squirming in their seats. They were beginning to feel somewhat uncomfortable as Ezekiel told them what he saw. They knew that God was speaking to them and their hypocrisy. Even spiritual leaders can live a lie, but they cannot hide that lie from God.

From this room filled with detestable animals and idols, the Lord brought the prophet out in his vision to the entrance of the north gate. Ezekiel looked and saw some women in the midst of a pagan ritual in honor of the Babylonian god Tammuz. Historians believe that Tammuz was a fertility god. Fertility gods were believed to be responsible for the harvest. Ezekiel was dismayed by what he saw (verse 14). How could these women have the audacity to worship a pagan god in the house of the Lord? As he grieved over this scene, the Lord told him that he had more to show him. They entered the inner court of the temple. There, twenty-five men with their backs toward the temple were bowing down to worship the sun in the east. Reference is made in verse 17 to "putting the branch to their nose." While we do not know exactly what this practice was, it is assumed that it too was a pagan, idolatrous practice. It may be of significance that their backs were toward the temple. In order for them to bow down and worship the sun, they were required to turn their backs on God. Notice that they were in the temple but turning their backs on God. This is a very sad picture but one that may very well be repeating itself in our day. It is quite possible to be in the house of the Lord and call yourself a believer and still have your back turned to God in rebellion. The idols we bow down to today may be different. Some bow down to the idol of materialism. Some bow to themselves and their pride. Some have fallen into the snare of worldliness. God was grieved by what he saw that day in the temple. He looked beyond the externals and saw the attitude of the heart. What does he see when he looks down on us?

The temple was filled with evil. This was a place that had been dedicated to the honor of God. It now brought him great dishonor. Here the people of God blasphemed his name by their evil practices. There are churches in our land today that are no different. These churches were, at one point in their history, dedicated to the glory of the Lord. Now they have stooped to the pagan practices of our day. They no longer bring glory to God. What does God see when he looks through the walls of your church? What does he see when he looks deep into your heart? It was not that God's people were not religious. They were still going to the temple and bringing their offerings. They had enough of God to comfort themselves, but they also bowed their knees to the pagan gods of their day. God saw right through their hypocrisy. Here he gave his prophet a glimpse of what was happening below the surface. I wonder what he sees today?

For Consideration:

- Is it possible that the church of our day is as guilty of hypocrisy as the people of God in the temple in Ezekiel's day? Give some examples.

- What kinds of gods are we guilty of bringing into our churches today?

- What do you think God sees as he looks at the church of our day?

- Is there anything we can really hide from God? How does this passage help us to answer this question?

For Prayer:

- Pray for your spiritual leaders. Ask God to give them sincere hearts free from all hypocrisy.

- Are there things that you do in the dark that no one knows about? What does this passage teach us? Ask God to set you free from those practices or sins.

- Take a moment to pray that God would expose any darkness in your church that is keeping it from growing.

9
Slaughter in the City

Read Ezekiel 9

In the last meditation we saw how the Lord brought the prophet Ezekiel, in a vision, to the city of Jerusalem where he showed him the city and the temple. Here God revealed the sin of the people in the temple of God. Because of this sin, they were driving God away. We see here in chapter 9 what would happen to those who had turned their backs on the Holy One of Israel.

In his vision the prophet Ezekiel heard a loud voice calling for those in charge of the city to approach. Notice in verse 1 that these individuals were commanded to approach with deadly weapons in hand. Ezekiel saw six men approach. Each of these men had a "battle-ax" in his hand (verse 2 NKJV). One man among them was dressed in linen and had a writing kit at his side.

Who were these men? They appear to be angels of God. We understand this from several important factors. First, they were the instruments that God used to bring judgment on his people for their sins. Second, the one with the writing kit marked those who lamented the evil in the city. This particular responsibility would not likely have been handed over to mere humans. Notice here that the angels had charge over the city. This tells us something about the ministry of angels. They are given charge over cities and individuals to carry out God's purposes.

Notice that these angels came and stood before the altar. The altar was where sacrifice was made for sin. They stood before the one symbol in the temple that represented the sin of God's people and the forgiveness that could have been theirs. As a people, however, Israel had rejected this offer of forgiveness. It was fitting, therefore, that this was the gathering point for these angels as they assembled to execute the judgment of God on his own people.

As Ezekiel watched, the glory of the Lord moved from the cherubim on the ark of the covenant to the threshold of the temple. In the days of the Old Testament, God revealed himself from between the wings of the cherubim on the ark of the covenant in the Holy of Holies. His presence was now being removed from the Holy of Holies. He stood at the threshold of the temple ready to leave. The sins of God's people had driven him from his own house.

Ezekiel heard the voice of the Lord call out to the angel who had the writing kit at his side. He commanded him to go out among the people and mark the foreheads of those who mourned because of the evil in the land. The mark on the forehead obviously was for the purpose of protection. God would not punish the righteous with the wicked. There was a separating out of the wheat and the tares. He separated his sheep from the goats. Notice here that it was those who grieved over the sin of the land that were marked. Would we be among them? There are times when we become so desensitized to what is happening around us that sin no longer seems to bother us. We no longer mourn and grieve over evil. God appears to take this very seriously. He is looking for a people who share his heart regarding sin.

Ezekiel heard the Lord command the angels with the deadly weapons to follow the angel with the writing kit and destroy all those who did not receive the mark on their foreheads. They were to show no pity but to utterly destroy all those who no longer grieved over sin in their midst. They were to kill both old and young, little children and women (verse 6).

Note that the Lord ordered his angelic servants to begin at the sanctuary. Why did he begin here? It was here we discovered that the name of the Lord was being blasphemed. These people had every opportunity to turn to God but they turned their backs on him. Notice in particular that the angels began their judgment with the elders of the temple. These were the leaders of God's people. Their judgment would be very severe. They should have led God's people into the truth of his Word, but instead they led them astray. This certainly reminds us as leaders of our great responsibility. Judgment will begin with us.

In verse 7 we see that God was not afraid to defile his own temple. He called his angels to go into the temple and fill the courts with the slain. What a surprise it would have been to the people of God to see God himself defile his own temple because of their sin. This place was no longer holy. It had already been defiled by the sinful actions of God's people in it.

The angels left on their mission of judgment. Ezekiel was left alone. He watched the men move out into the city, killing the inhabitants. It is hard to imagine what was going through his mind as he watched the horror before him. Men, women, children, and old folk were being stuck by the battle-ax of God's judgment. Bodies lay scattered throughout the city. As he watched this terrible scene before him, Ezekiel was afraid that the whole land would be destroyed. He questioned God on this matter. He asked him if he was going to destroy the whole city (verse 8). Underneath this was a certain doubt in the mind of Ezekiel about the justice of what God was doing. God reminded him in verse 9 that their punishment was just. The land was filled with violence and bloodshed. They had turned their backs on God.

As Ezekiel spoke with the Lord God about this matter, the angel with the writing kit returned to say that he had completed his task. The judgment was final. There could be no changing it now. There would be no more chances.

The scene before us is a reminder of the holiness and justice of God. Sin is an abomination in the eyes of God. He does not treat it lightly. The day is coming when the Lord God will judge sin. He will show no mercy on that day. Now is the time to repent. Now is the time to come to him before it is too late.

For Consideration:

- Are we, as believers, lowering our standard and accepting sin more and more? Explain.

- What do you suppose is causing us not to grieve like God grieves over sin today?

- What does this chapter teach us about the reality of the judgment of God?

- A sign of our love for God is that we grieve when we know his heart is broken. Do you agree with this statement or not? Explain. What does this mean for you personally?

For Prayer:

- Ask God to give you his mind and heart as it relates to sin.

- Ask him to forgive you for the times when you have not been concerned about the sin around you.

- Ask God to raise up a generation of believers who will fight for holiness and righteousness in the land.

10

Glory Departed

Read Ezekiel 10

In chapter 8 we caught a glimpse of the temple from the perspective of the Lord. We saw how the people were worshiping other gods in the temple of God. This had provoked the Lord to jealousy. He sent his angels throughout the city to slaughter those who did not grieve over the sins of the nation. Ezekiel was moved by what he saw that day. He wondered if anyone would be left in Jerusalem when the judgment of God was complete.

As Ezekiel looked around in his vision, he noticed some cherubim. We will say something more about these angels at a later point. Above the heads of these cherubim, Ezekiel noticed a great throne which appeared to be made of sapphire. Obviously, this was a very spectacular throne. In chapter 1 Ezekiel saw four creatures, each with four faces and four wings. Obviously, the creatures of chapter 1 were angelic creatures, just like the cherubim in this chapter. Above the creatures of chapter 1, Ezekiel saw this very same throne (see Ezekiel 1:26).

As he listened, Ezekiel heard a voice from the throne crying out to the man clothed in linen. We met this man in chapter 9. He was the one who carried the writing kit and marked the foreheads of those who grieved for sin (see Ezekiel 9:2). This man was commanded to go in among the wheels under the cherubim and gather some burning coals. He was to scatter them around the city. These coals appear to represent the judgment of God.

It is important to note that these angelic beings, according to Ezekiel 1:4–5, were engulfed in raging fire. We can assume that the task of entering into the wheels was not taken lightly. The man in linen moved into the flames to gather the coals as he had been commanded. Notice in verse 2 that the man was to fill his hands with these coals. Generally, coals would burn the hands. This man was protected from being burned. God will never call us to do something that he will not equip us to do by his strength. He will protect us as we move out in obedience, even as he protected this man in linen. The imagery here reminds us of Moses entering into the presence of God without being destroyed.

As the man went into the center of the wheels, the inner court of the temple was filled with a great cloud. The glory of the Lord moved up from the cherubim and paused over the threshold of the house of God. All around, Ezekiel could see the manifestation of the glory of God. He listened and heard the sound of the wings of the cherubim. This was a holy moment. The wings of the cherubim sounded like the voice of the Lord. This may simply be a reference to the sense of awe that this sound inspired.

Ezekiel then heard the voice of the Lord commanding the man in linen to take fire from "among the wheels, from among the cherubim" (verse 6). As Ezekiel watched, one of the cherubim reached out and gathered some coals and placed them in the hands of the man dressed in linen. He noted in verse 8 that the cherubim appeared to have the hands of a man under their wings. The man in linen took the fire and went out.

Ezekiel's attention then focused on the cherubim. He described them in greater detail in verses 9–17. Let's take a moment to consider these cherubim. The prophet noticed first that there was a wheel by each of the cherubim. These wheels appeared to have the color of a beryl stone. Beryl is light green in color. These wheels were the same as the wheels of chapter 1. Each of the wheels was like a wheel intersecting a wheel. These wheels, because of their construction, could move in any one of the four directions (north, south, east, or west). Ezekiel noticed next that the bodies of these cherubim and the wheels were full of eyes. They had a special ability to see everywhere. Another important detail about the cherubim was that they each had four faces. Each had the face of a cherub, a man, a lion, and an eagle. These are the faces of the greatest of all the creation of God. The cherub represented the celestial creation of God. Man represented the king of the earthly creation of God. The lion was the king of the wild animals. The eagle was the king of the birds. They were powerful and intelligent creatures. In verse 15 Ezekiel noted that these cherubim were the same creatures he saw at the Kebar River in chapter 1. He also stated in verse 20 that the throne he saw was the throne of the God of Israel.

Verse 22 poses somewhat of a problem for us. Ezekiel noticed that the faces he saw in chapter 10 were the same as the faces on the creatures he saw by the Kebar River. At the Kebar River in chapter 1, the prophet described four creatures who had the faces of a man, an ox, a lion, and an eagle. In chapter 10, however, the cherubim did not have the face of an ox. This face had been replaced with the face of a cherub. Why did the prophet tell us here that the faces were the same? Commentators are perplexed with this verse. Explanations range from stating that the face of the cherub looked like an ox to claiming an error on the part of the scribes who copied these manuscripts. While we do not have a clear explanation of this difference, Ezekiel made his point. These cherubim were the same as the cherubim he met in chapter 1.

There is a close connection between the wheels and the cherubim. The spirit of the cherubim was in the wheels. Wherever the wheels went, so did the cherubim and vice versa. These angelic beings were not their own. They were being led by a power outside of themselves. They were completely at the disposal of these wheels. Their spirit was in these wheels. There is a sense here in which we too are to be like these angelic beings. We have been bought by the Lord Jesus. We are his servants. We have given up our own rights. We are now called to live and move in obedience to his leading and prompting, like these cherubim.

When the man dressed in linen took the fire from the cherub, the glory of the Lord departed from the threshold of the temple. It moved above the cherubim. In verse 19 the cherubim themselves moved up from the earth and the temple toward heaven. As they moved upward, the glory of the Lord departed with them until God's presence was no longer in the temple. The sins of the people had driven him away. They had been judged and were now left to their evil ways.

What a sad picture is painted for us in these chapters. God's presence was no longer with his people. They had been judged because of their sin. Their evil practices had driven his presence from them. Could this picture be a warning to us today? The New Testament teaches us that our bodies are the temples of the Lord. When the Lord looks into your temple, what does he see? Does he see what he saw in the temple of Jerusalem? Is your temple dedicated to the honor of the Lord Jesus? Is he pleased with what he discovers in the hidden recesses of your mind and heart? You alone can answer these questions. Do not take Ezekiel's prophecy lightly. Revelation 3:20 speaks of the Lord Jesus standing at the door of the church seeking admission. He should have been already inside the church, but the Laodiceans had driven him away by their sin. Have you been doing the same? It is true that God promises that he will never leave us or forsake us. It is important for us to understand, however, that while God will not abandon us personally, his glory and empowerment *can* leave us. There are many believers today who are living as powerless believers. They do not reflect the glory of God in their lives. There is in reality very little difference between them and the unbeliever beside them. They are not being filled daily with God's Spirit. They are trying to live the Christian life by themselves. They have in fact driven God from their lives, though they still call upon his name. What a difference it makes, however, when the presence of the Lord is powerfully with us. People see the difference and are struck by that difference.

Have you shut God out of your life? Have you driven his glory and empowerment away by your sin? Confess this to him today. Open your heart to him in obedience. Let him fill you to overflowing again. Don't let what happened to the temple of God happen to you.

For Consideration:

* Is it possible for the glory of God and his empowering to leave our churches and our personal lives without God himself forsaking us? Explain.

* Can you think of examples of individuals who lost the sense of God's empowerment and glory in their lives because of sin? Did God forsake them during this time?

* What is the difference between people who are filled with the Spirit of God and those who are trying to live the

Christian life by their own efforts?

For Prayer:

- Moses once prayed that God would show him his glory. He knew that his experience of God was not complete. He wanted to know more of his glory in his life. Would you like to pray that prayer today?

- What is it that hinders you from experiencing God at a deeper level in your life today? Ask God to reveal these obstacles to you today.

11

The Caldron

Read Ezekiel 11

We should not assume that every Christian leader is a man or woman of God. There are those who carry the title but are not true servants. In Ezekiel 11 the Spirit of the Lord brought the prophet Ezekiel to the east gate of the temple. Here the prophet met twenty-five men. We have already seen these men in Ezekiel 8:16. They were in the entrance to the temple with their backs to the temple worshiping the sun. Even though these men were found in the temple, they were evil men. They were not concerned about the ways of the Lord. The Bible tells us that they were "giving wicked advice in the city" (verse 2).

What was the counsel they were giving to the people of God? Verse 3 tells us: "They say, 'Will it not soon be time to build houses? This city is a cooking pot, and we are the meat.'" This is a very difficult verse to understand. What were these men really saying? Let us consider first the illustration of the cooking pot. It is interesting to note that

Ezekiel had already used a similar illustration in this book. In Ezekiel 4:3 the prophet was commanded by the Lord to take an iron pan (a cooking pot of sorts) and place it over the picture of the Jerusalem etched in the clay tablet. This symbolized the fact that the city would be surrounded by her enemies. Is it possible that these twenty-five men took the illustration of Ezekiel and twisted it to justify their evil deeds? "Yes," they may have said to themselves, "we are, as Ezekiel has told us, inside this cooking pot. Does that not prove, however, that we will be safe and secure? Won't the walls of that pot protect us from the enemy?" Ezekiel's pot illustrated the judgment of God. Their pot falsely illustrated peace and security.

In verse 3 these men spoke about building houses. There has been some difficulty here in the translation of this verse. The NIV says: "Will it not soon be time to build houses?" The NKJV translates: "*The time is* not near to build houses"; the words "the time is" are in italics, indicating that these words are not in the original language but are needed in English to make sense of the verse. This leaves us with a problem interpreting this verse. Did these individuals counsel the people to build houses or not? The answer depends on how you translate the verse from the original language. We understand that the counsel that these men were giving the people was evil. If they were counseling them to build houses, the idea here is that they did not really believe that the judgment of God was near. They encouraged God's people to continue to live as they were living. If, on the other hand, the counsel here was not to build houses, the understanding could be that they did not have to build any kind of protection to keep themselves from the coming enemy. In either case, the leaders were expressing doubt about the prophecy of doom and gloom. They provided the people with a sense of false security.

The prophet Jeremiah also prophesied against leaders

like this: "From the least to the greatest, all are greedy for gain; prophets and priests alike, all practice deceit. They dress the wound of my people as though it were not serious. 'Peace, peace,' they say, when there is no peace" (Jeremiah 6:13–14). The prophets in Jeremiah's day also deceived the people into thinking that everything was all right. In actual fact, however, things were very wrong.

We cannot afford to be so deceived. There are false prophets in our day. They preach of a God of love who would never send a person to hell. They proclaim that there is a place in heaven for everyone. They proclaim that all religions lead to God. This is not the message of the Word of God. Do not be deceived. There is only one measure of truth. The Word of God, as found in the Holy Scriptures, is our only reliable guide.

God was not deaf to the things that were being said in Ezekiel's day. He knows the thoughts of our minds (verse 5). He saw how his people had filled the streets with the slain. They felt that because they were in the cooking pot of the holy city, they would be safe from harm. Ezekiel warned them that this was not the case. In verse 7 God told his people that he would take them out of their walled city. He would take them from the protection of their cooking pot. They would fall by the sword they feared. God would not allow the walls of the great city of Jerusalem to hinder him from exercising his righteous judgment on his people. In verse 9 Ezekiel told them that they would be delivered up to strangers who would conquer them. No longer would the city be their caldron, nor would they be the choice meat in the caldron (verse 11). They were under a false hope. They would lose everything.

What do you trust in today? What is your "cooking pot"? For some it is their Christian family. For others it is their church. Still others believe that if they do enough good deeds, they will be accepted. Do not be deceived, like the people of Ezekiel's day, into thinking that any of these things will keep you from the judgment of God. Only the blood of Christ is sufficient to pardon and forgive.

Even while Ezekiel was prophesying, the Lord gave the people a sign. One of the twenty-five leaders was struck dead by the Lord (verse 13). This was a small foretaste of what was to come. Ezekiel himself was struck by the power of the Lord demonstrated that day. The people listening to the prophet could not help but listen more carefully. God had given them a sign. To refuse this sign would be foolish indeed.

After these events, the Lord again spoke through Ezekiel. He reminded him that, while he was going to judge his people for their sin, he would not forsake them. Even though they would be scattered to the far corners of the earth, God would still be with them. He promised in verse 16 that he would be a sanctuary for his scattered people. Even in discipline, we see the grace and compassion of God. He also told the prophet that after he had punished his people, they would be restored. Ezekiel prophesied that these scattered people would return again to Jerusalem (verse 17). This would take place some years later under Nehemiah and Ezra.

On that day when God would restore his people, they would receive a new heart and a new spirit. There would be a movement of God's Spirit among them. They would remove the detestable things in the land. They would walk in the ways of the Lord. God would take away their stony heart and replace it with a soft heart of flesh (verse 19). Those who refused the ways of the Lord would be judged and he would bring down the deeds they had done on their own heads.

It is important for us to note here that even when the children of Israel returned under Ezra and Nehemiah, they really did not receive this new heart and new spirit. This leads us to understand that, while there would be a partial fulfillment of this prophecy in the days of Ezra and

Nehemiah, there was an even greater fulfillment to come. That fulfillment would ultimately come through the Lord Jesus who would give his people a new heart and put his Holy Spirit in them. Ezekiel looked forward to a day when God would move in revival among his own people. We have yet to see the complete fulfillment of this prophecy in the life of Israel. There is a sense, however, that we are seeing the fulfillment of Ezekiel's prophecy in the church of our day. Paul spoke of the church as a spiritual Israel (Romans 9:6–8). We are seeing God break stony hearts in our day. We are seeing him fill his people with his Holy Spirit and equip them to live as Christ would have them live.

As Ezekiel was prophesying, the glory of the Lord was lifted up to the top of the mountain high above the people of Israel. God distanced himself from his people. Their sins and rebellion had driven him far from them, but he would return when he had dealt with their sin. He would not forsake them. After this, Ezekiel's vision ended, and he found himself among the people of God in Babylon. He shared with them what he had seen in his vision.

What is the challenge of this chapter to us in our day? Despite what Israel's leaders were saying, things were not right. God was angry with his people. This chapter tells us that even spiritual leaders may be misguided. They may be sincere people. They may be good-living and nice people, but this is not a guarantee that they know the truth of the Word of God. Ezekiel came into conflict with the leaders of his day. God's people were hearing conflicting messages. There are many messages being preached in our day as well. Our only authoritative guide is the Word of God. Do not be deceived by those who preach a false message. Examine the Word of God for yourself. Examine what you hear from the pulpit in light of the Word of God. Submit your own beliefs to a careful examination. Let the Word of God alone be your guide.

For Consideration:

- Why is it so easy for false teachers in our day to prosper?

- Why have the cults been so successful in drawing people away from the clear teaching of the Word of God? Why were the false prophets successful in this chapter?

- What are our "caldrons" today? What do people trust in for salvation and assurance of heaven?

For Prayer:

- Are there Christian churches in your area that are giving their members a false security? Pray that God would do a work of grace in their midst.

- Are you sure of your salvation? Ask God to reveal any "caldrons" in your life that you are trusting to give you favor with God.

- Ask God for an opportunity to share the message of salvation through Christ with someone in the next week.

12

A False Israelite Proverb

Read Ezekiel 12

If you knew that the Lord was returning today, would you change anything in your life? We continue in sin, not because we do not know that what we do is wrong, but because we feel that we still have time to make it right before having to answer to the Lord. Ezekiel 12 challenges this mentality. This was the mentality of the people of Israel. They were a rebellious people. They had closed their eyes and ears to the words of the prophets God had sent to them. Seeing that his people would no longer listen to his words, God called Ezekiel to act out his message visually before them.

In Ezekiel 12 the Lord God asked the prophet Ezekiel to pack his belongings as though he were going into exile. He was to do this in the sight of the people of Israel. He was to pack his belongings during the day, and in the evening he was to put them on his shoulders and leave the city as though he were being led out into captivity (verse 4). The reason for acting out this message was clear: "It may be that they will consider, though they are a rebellious house" (verse 3 NKJV). If they would not listen to a sermon, then maybe they would listen to a skit. The method was not important. What *was* important was that the message be communicated in a way the people would understand.

Notice here that Ezekiel's means of leaving the city was somewhat peculiar. He was to dig a hole in the wall, in the presence of the people, and leave the city through this hole (verse 5). As he walked through the city, he was to carry his belongings on his shoulders and cover his face. Why does he cover his face? From verse 10 we see that this action symbolized what would happen to their king. The Bible tells us in 2 Kings 25:3–7 that Zedekiah, the prince of Jerusalem at the time of the exile, would have his eyes put out so that he would not be able to see. The prince of Jerusalem would escape through a hole in the wall, bearing his belongings on his shoulders. Notice here in verse 12 that, though the prince would attempt an escape, God would spread his net over him and bring him to the land of the Chaldeans (Babylon). As for his troops, they would be scattered to the wind. This was exactly what happened to King Zedekiah. Verse 12 goes on to say that though this prince would live in the land of the Chaldeans and eventually die there, he would never see it. This is clearly a reference to the fact that the Babylonians would pluck out his eyes and make him blind. A comparison of this prophecy with the account of the exile shows us that these things happened exactly as Ezekiel said. Compare the following passage with what Ezekiel had been prophesying:

> By the ninth day of the fourth month the *famine in the city* had become so severe that there was no food for the people to eat. Then the city wall was broken through, and the whole *army fled at night through the gate between the two walls* near the king's garden,

though the Babylonians were surrounding the city. They fled toward the Arabah, but *the Babylonian army pursued the king and overtook him* in the plains of Jericho. *All his soldiers were separated from him and scattered,* and he was captured. He was taken to the king of Babylon at Riblah, where sentence was pronounced on him. They killed the sons of Zedekiah before his eyes. *Then they put out his eyes, bound him with bronze shackles and took him to Babylon.* (2 Kings 25:3–7, emphasis mine)

We learn in verse 15 that in the day of God's wrath, his people would be scattered to the four corners of the earth. Many would lose their lives and perish by the sword of their enemy. God would spare a remnant among them, however, so that they would be able to recount the story of God's judgment to future generations.

In verse 18 God asked the prophet Ezekiel to eat and drink with trembling. This was because the people of Israel would eat and drink in anxiety and despair because of what they saw happening all around them. Their towns would be wasted. Their land would be devastated. They would be surrounded by violence and doom. When they saw these things happening around them, they would know that there was a God in Israel. They would also recognize that they had offended him. The Bible tells us that one day every knee will bow and recognize that Jesus is Lord (Philippians 2:10–11). Even those who doubt him will one day know that he is Lord. For the Israelites of Ezekiel's day, however, it was too late. Their judgment had already come. Don't wait until it is too late. Come to him now.

Notice the response of the people to the words of the prophet. They had a proverb that went something like this: "The days go by and every vision comes to nothing" (verse 22). This proverb shows us the state of Israel's faith. Who had visions in the land of Israel? Was it not the prophets? What these people were saying is this: "Day after day goes by and yet what the prophets tell us never happens. Their visions never come to pass." Listen to what they were saying in verse 27: "The vision he sees is for many years from now, and he prophesies about the distant future."

These people did not worry about what the prophets were saying. They did not feel that what Ezekiel was telling them would happen in their lifetime. They had lots of time to make things right with God. This was the mentality of the day.

In response to this attitude of the people, God told Ezekiel that this proverb would shortly be replaced by another proverb: "The days are near when every vision will be fulfilled" (verse 23). Yes, the day was coming when the visions of the prophets would come to pass. The vision of Ezekiel and his fellow prophets concerning the destruction of Jerusalem was not very far away. God reminded his people in verse 28 that his words would no longer be postponed. Now was the time that God would bring these words to pass. Now was the day of judgment. God's people did not have the time they thought they had. He would call on them to give an account of their actions sooner then they thought.

Does this chapter not cause us to reflect upon our own spiritual condition? There are many people in our day who are living in sin. They have every intention of making things right with the Lord—but not yet. They want a few more years to live before making any changes. In many ways, they are like the people of Israel. They know that the Lord is coming and will call them to repentance. They feel, however, that they have plenty of time before they will have to answer to Him. If this is your situation, let me remind you of the uncertainty of life. Your life could be cut short at any moment. The Lord Jesus could come at any moment. If he called you to himself today, would you be ready to face him? All of us need to live our lives in such a way that we are always ready for the coming of the Lord. You may not have the time you think you have. You could be called home today. Remember that God said to Ezekiel the day was coming when the words of the prophets would be fulfilled. Will you be ready?

For Consideration:

- God seems to be encouraging creativity in the presentation of Ezekiel's message by asking him to act it out. Not everyone is gifted in the same way. How can you creatively present the gospel to those around you?

- Why do you suppose we tend to keep putting off our decisions to make the necessary changes in our lives?

- What would you change if you knew that this was your last day on earth?

For Prayer:

- Ask God to help you be faithful in using the gifts he has given you to reach out to others.

- Ask God to help you make the best use of the time he has given you on this earth.

- If you have never accepted the Lord Jesus as your Savior, don't waste another moment of your life. Surrender to his will. Accept the forgiveness he offers you today.

13

Whitewashed Walls

Read Ezekiel 13

In chapter 11 Ezekiel was called to confront the spiritual leaders of his day because of their false teaching. While these leaders came across very convincingly, God compared them here to whitewashed walls. They looked good on the outside, but underneath they were full of flaws and cracks.

These men and women were prophesying "out of their own heart" (verse 2 NKJV). They were preaching their own opinions. They were not concerned about God's Word. Their message did not come from the Lord. Verse 3 tells us that these prophets "followed their own spirit." The authoritative Word of God was taking second place to the ideas of people. Have things changed in our day?

If you have ever had an opportunity to preach or teach, you know how easy it is to fall into this trap. You do not have to preach or teach heresy to fall prey to this temptation. It is quite possible to preach the truth in such a way that it focuses people's attention on the preacher and not on what God wants to communicate to his people. How often have I found myself standing in front of God's people without truly seeking to know what God would have me communicate to them. Instead, I have shared my own intellectual insights on a given passage. We too can be guilty of prophesying *out of our own hearts* rather than the particular word of God for his people.

The prophets were compared here to foxes in the desert. This expression is difficult to understand. The fox was noted for being very sly and cunning. He was also known for the destruction he caused. This was what these prophets were like. By deceit and falsehood they fed themselves at the expense of others. The fact that these foxes were in the deserts would make them even more cunning and sly (since their food would be very scarce).

The second accusation God brought against these prophets was that they did not repair the gaps (verse 5). Reference was being made here to the city wall. The enemy had been attacking the people of God. They had been successful in piercing their wall of faith. The prophets were not concerned that the faith of the people was being eroded. It did not overly distress them that falsehood was creeping into the lives of the people of God. They did not strengthen the people to face the enemy. They did not teach the truth. They left these gaps in the wall wide open. This was an open invitation for the enemy.

In our day we must not stand idly by while the wall of sound doctrine is being battered by the attacks of the enemy. We cannot watch our brothers and sisters wander from the truth without doing something to bring them back. We must put aside our concerns about our own reputations and what people think of us. We cannot afford to go with the flow when God calls us to stand firm for his truth.

Ezekiel tells us that these false prophets introduced their

prophecies by saying: "Thus says the Lord" (verse 6 NKJV). What they preached, however, did not come from the Lord. They had a religious language. They spoke of God and of faith, but they were not God's messengers. They were his enemies. The Lord was against them because they led his people astray. They proclaimed nonsense and foolishness (verses 7–8).

We see in verse 9 that, because these false prophets and teachers had spoken lies in God's name, the hand of God would be against them. They would no longer be welcome in the assembly of God's people. God would remove them from the land. Every record of their presence would be erased. These false prophets would be banished. They considered themselves to be servants of God, but they were his enemies. Because of them God's people were wandering dangerously from the fold. They would have to answer to God for how they had misled his people. God would deal with them before they caused more damage.

God accused these prophets in verse 10 of seducing his people. They had been proclaiming peace when there was no peace. They were like those who whitewashed a wall that was full of cracks and holes. Israel was like that crumbling wall. The nation needed major repairs. The prophets downplayed the seriousness of the nation's spiritual problems. They did not point people to their sin. They offered them false consolation and hope. They told them that everything would be all right when in reality the judgment of God was about to fall.

What a sad day that would be for the people of God! Men and women had put their confidence in these prophets. Their eternal destiny was based on what these false prophets proclaimed. As they stood before God, they would realize that they had been deceived. For many it would be too late. God would rain his judgment on their whitewashed wall. God would rain his judgment on their whitewashed wall and it would come crashing down.

The deception that was taking place in Israel was not only on the part of the male prophets. The women, as well, were leading people astray. Among the women of Israel were those who made magic charms for the wrists and veils for the heads (verse 18). These articles were used in some form of pagan ritual. The nature of these rituals is uncertain. Verse 18 tells us that these women would "hunt" (NKJV) or "ensnare" (NIV) the souls of God's people. These women would not escape God's judgment. They would be punished for their evil deeds. God wants us to separate from the evil practices of false religions.

I remember when we worked on the Island of Reunion in the Indian Ocean. The leaders would go with a new believer to his home. They would go through all his belongings and take away all the articles that were used in the worship of false gods. Together with the leaders of the church, they would go to the ocean and there, after some prayer, they would throw all these religious articles in the ocean. They separated themselves completely from their former false religion. This is what the Lord God expected of his people in Israel. They were to throw away their magic charms and veils that were used in the worship of their false gods. He expects the same of us today.

Notice how justice was being perverted in verse 19. For a handful of barley and bread, those who should have died were granted liberty, and those who should have been set free were condemned to death. There was no justice. Bribes were common in the land. If you had money, you could get away with your crime. If you didn't have money to pay off the judges, you would be punished, even for things you did not do. God saw these things in the land. These deeds would not go unpunished.

God reminded his people in verses 20–21 that he would rip the magic charms from their arms and set free the souls they had ensnared. These women had been misleading others by their pagan practices. Those who came to them were being caught in their snares. They were being deceived into these false practices. This false teaching saddened the heart of the righteous in the land.

These false teachers had strengthened the hand of the wicked. God would not allow this to continue. Even his own people were being caught up in the evil influences of these false prophets and teachers. God knew those who were his. He would set them free from the hands of these false prophets (verse 23). He loved his own too much to see them perish at the hands of those who proclaimed falsehood.

How we need to pray today that God would release his people from the hands of these false prophets in our day. All too many are unaware of the deception that is taking place in their churches. Tradition and pride bind many. God promised here to set his people free. What encouragement we receive from this today. Even among those who are currently being deceived by false religions and cults are those whom God will reach and bring to himself.

Even in our day many false prophets and cults exist. They come across as being very spiritual. We are not to be deceived by their religious words. They are like whitewashed walls. On the outside they seem to be very sincere, but inside they are full of hypocrisy and deceit. May God give us great discernment to recognize these false prophets.

For Consideration:

• Do you suppose that the false prophets in our day sincerely believe that they are teaching the truth?

• Do you see people around you trapped in the doctrine of these false prophets? What comfort do you receive from this passage?

- How can we tell when someone is a true prophet of the Lord?

- What does this passage teach us about casting off the practices and articles of false religions? Why is this so important?

For Prayer:

- Do you know some people who are religious but lost? Take a moment to pray for them. Ask God to show them their need of the Savior.

- Pray for the false prophets of our day. Ask God to open up their hearts to the understanding of the truth.

- Pray for those true believers caught in the web of false teaching. In this chapter God promised to set them free. Take him at his word and pray that he would set them free.

14
Godly Fathers, Ruined Children

Read Ezekiel 14

There are people who hold on to their upbringing to get them to heaven. The fact that you were brought up in a good Christian home does not guarantee you a place in heaven. You can be part of a church that preaches the Word of God and still be spiritually lost. Each person is individually accountable to God for his or her own life. You cannot go to heaven on someone else's shoulders.

In Ezekiel 14 the elders of Israel came to inquire of the prophet Ezekiel. These elders were not the men they should have been. The Lord revealed to the prophet in verse 3 that they had set up idols in their hearts. Does it surprise you that these men served idols and yet came to inquire of the prophet? Is this not a common practice in our day? Are there not many who worship on Sunday who blaspheme his name during the week? This is what these elders were doing.

The Lord asked Ezekiel if he should allow these elders to come to him with their problems (verse 3). While God was not obliged to speak to these leaders, because their hearts were far from him, he did give Ezekiel a message for them. In verse 6 God told them to repent and turn from their idols. If they did not turn from their idols, God would turn his face against them and cut them off from his people (verse 8). God got straight to the point. He knew their hearts and would soon judge them if they did not repent.

In verses 9 and 10 God explained that the punishment for false prophets who did not speak the word of the Lord would be the same as those who listened to them. False prophets would not be able to hide behind their positions. They would perish like the other people because of their rebellion against God. There was a purpose behind this judgment. Notice in verses 5 and 11 that God would punish them so that they would return to him. He wanted to be their God and pour out his love on them. There were, however, obstacles in their relationship. God told Ezekiel that he would cut off their supply of bread (verses 12–13). Some would even perish under the heavy discipline of the Lord. God would not allow them to continue wandering from him and blaspheming his name. He would do whatever it took to break this rebellion and bring them back to himself. Maybe you have experienced some of this discipline in your life. The discipline of the Lord is never easy. What a blessing it is, however, to know that God loves us enough to fight for us.

God was going to bring his judgment upon the false prophets of the land (verse 9). God would entice them to prophesy. Then he would destroy them. What is happening here? Why would God entice these individuals to prophesy when he knew that the words they spoke were false? What we need to understand here is that God will not always remove every temptation from us. Even the Lord Jesus himself had to face temptation in his ministry. He faced Satan head on and was tempted by him for forty days. While God will not always remove every temptation from us, we can be sure that he will use whatever temptation we face to bring us closer to himself. Sometimes these temptations are designed to test us and reveal our true quality. In this case these prophets were being tested. Just like Jesus, they were faced with the opportunity to sin and turn their backs on God. Just like Adam and Eve in the Garden of Eden, they stood before an opportunity to sin. God enticed them in that he allowed this temptation to come before them. He wanted to know the quality of their hearts. The Lord did not stop these prophets from speaking lies. He allowed them to speak their own visions. He did not restrain them. He allowed them to speak their evil but would judge them for it.

We need to see here that the Lord will allow us at times to face temptations. He will not always stop temptations from coming our way. We will have to face these temptations each and every day. The question is what will we do with these temptations? I have met individuals who believed that if God really wanted them to have victory in a certain situation, he would remove the temptation. This is not always the case. There are times when the Lord God calls us to run from those temptations ourselves. The prophets here in the days of Ezekiel failed the test because they did not run from the temptations that came their way.

When the Lord judged the people of Israel, not even Noah, Daniel, or Job would have been able to plead for their own children (verse 14). What do we know about these three men that helps us understand why God would mention them in particular here in this verse? The Bible says about Noah: "But Noah found favor in the eyes of the LORD. This is the account of Noah. Noah was a righteous man, blameless among the people of his time, and he walked with God" (Genesis 6:8–9).

Noah was a just man and faithful to the Lord. There was no one like him in his generation. When God's anger was poured out upon the earth through the flood in the days of

Noah, he and his family alone escaped the judgment of God. Through Noah, the seed of humanity was saved.

Concerning Daniel, we read: "At this, the administrators and the satraps tried to find grounds for charges against Daniel in his conduct of government affairs, but they were unable to do so. They could find no corruption in him, because he was trustworthy and neither corrupt nor negligent. Finally these men said, 'We will never find any basis for charges against this man Daniel unless it has something to do with the law of his God'" (Daniel 6:4–5). When the princes tried to find fault with Daniel, they could find none. If they were going to convict him of something, they would have to do so on the basis of his relationship with God.

In regard to Job, God himself said to Satan: "Have you considered my servant Job? There is no one on earth like him; he is blameless and upright, a man who fears God and shuns evil" (Job 1:8). In God's own words, there was not a person like Job on the surface of the earth. Here was a man that God himself considered to be faithful and upright.

Noah, Daniel, and Job, mentioned here in this chapter, were men of exemplary character. God told his people through Ezekiel that even if these men could plead for Israel, they would not be able to save the nation from the coming judgment. If God were to send a famine on the land to destroy men and animals, these men would escape alone. They could take no one with them. If God were to send wild beasts, these men, as righteous as they were, would not even be able to save their own families. If God sent the sword to kill the men and animals of the land, the sons and daughters of these three righteous men would perish if they did not repent of their sin. If God were to send a plague, these men alone would escape because of their right relationship with God.

God was going to send all four of these judgments upon the land of Israel. The punishment would be severe. God's people could not count on someone else interceding for them. The survivors of this great judgment would learn an important lesson. They would learn that they were individually accountable to God for their own sins. Daniel's children would have perished had they been living in Jerusalem at that time and had not turned to God. The faith of Noah would not have saved his children. The same could be said about Job.

This chapter teaches us that we must all individually give an account before God. These three men of God could not have helped even their own children to escape the judgment of God. You may have been brought up in the home of a Noah or a Daniel. Your parents may have been sincere people of God. You may attend a church that preaches the Word of God. You may surround yourself with men and women who love the Lord. Like the children mentioned here in our passage, however, your Christian upbringing will not save you. You can have Christian parents and still perish in your sins. Your Christian friends will be powerless to do anything for you in the day of judgment. There is no saint who can plead your case before God when he pours out his wrath. You will stand alone before God to give an accounting.

God's wrath was very real. Ezekiel reminds us that God would not destroy the entire nation. He would leave a remnant. The day was coming when God would move again in a very special way in the lives of this remnant. Through them he would remind the nation of her need to be right with God. Ezekiel was part of that remnant. We have his record of what God spoke to his people. We have an account of his warning and judgment. Through Ezekiel, God reminds us that one day we too will stand alone before a Holy God to give an account of our lives. Don't trust others. Don't rely upon your church or your spiritual leaders. The Lord Jesus alone can save you from your sins. You must come to him personally.

For Consideration:

- What do we learn here about the desire of God for a personal relationship with his people?

- What things do we trust in today to get us to heaven?

- Have you made a personal decision to follow the Lord Jesus? No one else can make this decision for you. Take a moment to consider if the faith you profess is really yours.

For Prayer:

- Do you know some people who are trusting in the wrong things to get to heaven? Take a moment to ask God to help them see the error of their ways.

- Thank God for giving you the assurance of your salvation through Jesus Christ alone.

- Ask him to search you now so that when you stand before him you will be unashamed.

15

A Useless Vine

Read Ezekiel 15

Have you ever seen a vine? How would you describe the wood of a vine? The first thing you notice about a vine is that it is very twisted. A vine is usually very long and thin. Because vines are fast growing plants, the wood is not strong. The wood of the vine serves no practical purpose. It is not big enough, strong enough, or straight enough to make any object for practical use. What would you think if your neighbor told you that he was going to build a house from the wood of a grapevine? Would you not consider him to be a fool?

Suppose we add another dimension to this illustration. Let us suppose that this wood has been removed from a fire. The ends are burned and the middle is charred. What could this wood be used for? In its natural state the wood could at least be used for decorative purposes. Now even that is impossible. The wood of a vine taken out of a fire is completely useless. The only purpose it could possibly serve would be as firewood.

Ezekiel told his people that they were like this charred vine. They were of no practical use to the Lord God. The only place for them would be in the fire of God's judgment. There in the fire they would be an example for others to see. Because of their sin, the Lord would set his face against them to consume them.

Let's consider this illustration in greater detail. How were God's people like this vine? First, remember that a vine is twisted and crooked. This was how God's people were. They were twisted and crooked like the vine because they were easily influenced by the circumstances around them. These people were driven from one false god to another. They were easily convinced to turn their backs on the one true God. Their foreign wives influenced them. They looked with envy upon the evil practices of their pagan neighbors. They served the Lord, and then turned to serve other gods. The road they followed was not straight and narrow. They moved from one side to another depending on the influence of the time. The result was that they were of no use to God.

Second, like the vine, the Israelites did not let the Lord strengthen them through adversity. When obstacles came their way, they moved around them. They did not set their minds on the Lord in their adversity. They did not commit themselves to move straight ahead through the obstacle by the strength of the Lord. They did not fix their eyes on the Lord and walk in his ways. Maybe you have seen how the roots of a tree can penetrate very hard substances. I have seen trees growing in the middle of a great rock. Somehow their roots are able to penetrate and find the nourishment they need. This is not the case for the vine. The vine grows very fast. Instead of moving through obstacles and allowing those obstacles to strengthen it, the vine simply moves around them. The result is a wood that has no physical strength. Israel was like the vine. She was weak and frail.

Third, a vine has a tendency to reach outward and not upward. The great trees of the forest direct their energies toward reaching for the skies. The Israelite tendency was not to send their shoots upward toward God but outward toward their neighbors. They looked more at what their pagan neighbors were doing than they looked toward God. Their faith was based not on the Word of the Lord but on the practices of their day. The result was a fruitless vine.

In God's eyes, Israel was a charred piece of vine. She was of no practical value to the Lord. Her sins had rendered her useless. What about you? Have you been like this vine? Have your sins rendered you useless to the Master? Despite the imperfections of a vine, it still can produce the most delightful of all fruits. Like this vine, we too have been warped and twisted by sin. We are never without hope, however. God can use us, twisted and weak as we are, to produce great fruit for his glory. This vine is in reality a picture of each of us. At best, we are like the wood of the vine. We are, in our natural state, of little use to God. God wants to take this vine, however, and do something wonderful with it. He wants to produce great fruit in you. Israel did not let God do this in her. Instead, she turned her back on God. How careful we need to be so we don't fall into the same error.

For Consideration:

• In what ways are we like the vine described in this passage?

• What significance do you see in the fact that the vine, with all its imperfections, can produce the greatest fruit? What encouragement do you take from this?

• What are your failures? How has God used you despite these failures?

For Prayer:

- Thank the Lord that despite our many imperfections, he can use us to produce much fruit.

- Ask the Lord to produce even more fruit through you for his glory.

16

Unfaithful Jerusalem

Read Ezekiel 16

Personally, I can think of no other passage in all of
Scripture that speaks as powerfully as Ezekiel 16.
You cannot read this chapter without being touched
deeply in your spirit. What we have here is a parable of
Jerusalem. This chapter shows us what was happening in the
land of Israel from God's perspective.

As we begin, Jerusalem is compared to an infant. This
infant was born in the land of the Canaanites. God had
promised Abraham that he would give to him the land of
the Canaanites: "On that day the Lord made a covenant
with Abram and said, 'To your descendants I give this land,
from the river of Egypt to the great river the Euphrates—the
land of the Kenites, Kenizzites, Kadmonites, Hittites,
Perizzites, Rephaites, Amorites, *Canaanites*, Girgashites
and Jebusites'" (Genesis 15:18–21, emphasis mine).

Later on in Egypt the Lord spoke to Moses. He reminded
him of his promise to Abraham, Isaac, and Jacob: "The LORD
said, 'I have indeed seen the misery of my people in Egypt.

I have heard them crying out because of their slave drivers, and I am concerned about their suffering. So I have come down to rescue them from the hand of the Egyptians and to bring them up out of that land into a good and spacious land, a land flowing with milk and honey—the home of the *Canaanites*, Hittites, Amorites, Perizzites, Hivites and Jebusites'" (Exodus 3:7–8, emphasis mine).

It was here in the land of the Canaanites that the nation of Israel was born. God reminded Israel that her father was an Amorite and her mother, a Hittite. There could possibly be two reasons why God said these nations were her parents: first, because the people of God inherited their land; second, because the people of God also inherited their evil practices. We can read about the sinfulness of the Amorites in Genesis 15:16. Listen to what Sarah told her husband, Abraham: "I am disgusted with living because of these Hittite women" (Genesis 27:46). Obviously, the practices of the Hittites left much to be desired. God's people inherited these sinful practices.

As a newborn child, Israel was left without her cord cut. She was not washed. No salt was applied to her to purify and kill the germs. No one wrapped her in cloth to cover her nakedness and provide warmth. She was left alone with no one to care for her. Ezekiel tells us that this newborn child was thrown into an open field with no protection or shelter and left to die.

This was her condition when the Lord God passed by. He saw Israel lying in her blood. He had compassion upon her. He reached out to her dying form and cried out, "Live!" He took her into his arms and cared for her until she had grown up. We should not underestimate the power of that word, "Live!" Who among us has not experienced something of that word in our own lives? God reaches out to us in our sin and helplessness and brings life. He gives us a reason to live. This little baby grew up to become a beautiful woman.

The Lord looked at her and loved her. He took her as his wife and entered into a covenant relationship with her. When she became his wife, God clothed her with the finest of clothes and jewelry. He fed her with the finest food. Her beauty became known throughout the world. She owed it all to God

In time, however, she began to trust in her beauty. She turned to prostitution, no longer satisfied with her own husband. She made male idols with the jewelry the Lord gave her. She clothed these idols with her embroidered clothes. She offered her fine food and oil as sacrifices to them. She even offered her sons and daughters, from her marriage with the Lord, in sacrifice to her foreign gods. Child sacrifice was a practice of the pagan nations around Israel. At times Israel would adopt this practice, and she too sacrificed her children on the altars of the land to the pagan gods of the surrounding nations. How this grieved God, her husband! She had forgotten what God had done for her.

It did not stop there. She built pagan shrines throughout the land. She preferred strangers to her husband. Ezekiel tells us that she was worse than a prostitute because she paid her lovers to come to her. They did not entice her. She gave herself freely to all the foreign nations around her. Her appetite for prostitution was out of control. She was never satisfied. She multiplied her acts of prostitution. Verse 27 tells us that even the daughters of the pagan Philistines were shocked at her behavior. Her heart was far from God. Her sin was greater than the nations around her.

God would not stand idly by while his wife rushed headfirst into sin and destruction. Out of love for her, he would strip her bare and expose her before her lovers. They would turn their backs on her. Out of jealousy for her (verse 38), God would break down her idols. As was the law of the day, she would be stoned and cut to pieces with the sword. Her house would be burned down. (This reference to the burning of her house may refer to what happened when her enemies came into Jerusalem and burned it to the ground.) She would be crushed because she did not remember what the Lord had done for her.

For generations to come, people would speak a proverb about Israel. They would say, "Like mother, like daughter" (see verse 44). To those women who turned away from their husbands, the people of the land would say that they were like their mother, Israel. She would come to represent evil and rebellion against God.

Ezekiel continued with his parable about Jerusalem by explaining that she had two sisters. One sister was named Samaria and the other, Sodom. Both of these cities were known for their evil. Sodom was known for its immorality during the days of Lot. Verse 49 described this city as being proud and full of idleness, refusing to help the poor and needy. For this reason, the city was destroyed. Samaria, as the capital of the northern kingdom of Israel, had turned her back on God under Jeroboam. Under his reign they established the worship of the golden calf in opposition to the worship of the God of their fathers. God told his people in verse 51 that even Samaria did not commit half the crimes God's wife, Jerusalem, was guilty of now. The worst part about it was that she was not even ashamed.

Jerusalem would be put to shame because of her evil. She would be taken into captivity. Before God humbled her, she looked down on her sisters, Samaria and Sodom. Verses 56 and 57 tell us that she would not even mention the names of her sisters. She considered herself to be better than they. The Jews of Ezekiel's time considered themselves to be the people of God and thus superior to the nations around them. Jerusalem looked down on the surrounding nations. Now, however, she would suffer the shameful consequences of her waywardness. Syria and Philistine would now look down on her. She was at one time the pride and beauty of the earth.

Now she would be put to shame before the astonished eyes of the unbelieving world.

Even in our day we have seen the uncovering of sin and shame in the lives of some who claimed to serve the Lord. They have been humbled, and their great spiritual kingdoms have toppled with them. How we need to take the warning of this chapter seriously! Let us never forget what the Lord has done for us. Let us always remember the pit from which we came.

Notice here that, though God must punish Jerusalem, he would not completely abandon her. Verses 60–63 tell us that, while she would be severely punished for her sins, God would remember his covenant with her. God would again pour out his Spirit upon her. He would again pick up her bloody and dying body and take her in his arms. He would cause her to remember the days of her youth when she was abandoned by all. God would remember his covenant with his unfaithful wife. He would pour out a spirit of repentance upon her. From this we understand that God may yet move in power in the Jewish nation. Ezekiel reminds us that God would return to Israel something of her former glory. She would be given the responsibility of caring for her rebellious sisters, Samaria and Sodom. Obviously, this was not because she had proven worthy of such a task. She would be given this responsibility simply because God is a God of grace who restores sinners to himself and gives them what they do not deserve.

What does this verse say to us in our churches today about those who have fallen, repented, and are now seeking to return to ministry? Is there not forgiveness for sin? When God forgives does he not forget and treat us as though we had never sinned? Even the apostle Paul was used of God in a mighty way. He persecuted the church, and yet God used him to become a great apostle. Peter denied the Lord but was chosen to be the instrument of God to reach three thousand souls on the day of Pentecost. David fell into the sin of adultery but was still a man after God's own heart. Praise God for his forgiveness. Praise him that he does not leave us in the stench of our rebellion.

How often we have tried God's patience. Maybe as you read, you are forced to look at your own life. Maybe you too, like this young child, were left to die. The world left you empty and destitute. You felt abandoned. The Lord Jesus had compassion on you. He reached out and picked you up out of the gutter. He clothed you with the richest of blessings. He loved you like you had never been loved before. He drew you to himself.

Today, however, you have lost that first love. The things of this world have tempted you. You have turned your back on him. Like the young wife in this chapter, you preferred strangers to your husband. Maybe the Lord is calling you to remember the pit from which you were removed (Psalm 40:2). Maybe he is calling you back to his side. Won't you return to him today? Won't you confess your wandering? He waits with arms open wide.

For Consideration:

- What does this chapter teach us about the compassion of God?

- Notice here how, despite the waywardness of Israel, God is willing to take her back to himself and forgive her of her sin. What does this teach us about those who wander from the Lord today?

- Can you identify with the wife in this chapter? How have you wandered from God? What blessings has he given you?

- What does this chapter teach us about how we need to treat those who have wandered from the Lord?

For Prayer:

- Thank the Lord that he did not give up on you even when you were not faithful to him.

- Take a moment to reflect on where you were without the Lord in your life. What has he done for you? Thank him for his grace.

- Ask God to give you patience with those who have not yet had victory over their sin and rebellion. Ask the Lord to help you to love them as he loves them.

17

The Eagle and the Vine

Read Ezekiel 17

There are times in our Christian walk when we do not understand the will of the Lord. The Lord may call us to walk in unpleasant places. The temptation is to be like Jonah and run in the opposite direction. Like Jonah, however, we find out how much easier it would have been to have obeyed. The people of Israel suffered much because they did not want to follow God's plan for their lives. They had other ideas. In this chapter God reminded his people of the dangers of rejecting him and his purposes.

We begin here with a parable of an eagle. This eagle was a beautiful bird. She was powerful. She had long and sturdy wings. Her feathers were long and full of many beautiful colors. In this passage she represented the king of Babylon (see verse 12).

This eagle came to Lebanon (representing the southern kingdom of Israel called Judah). She broke off the "top of a cedar" (verse 3) and brought it to a land of merchants and traders. In 2 Kings 24:8 we read that when King Jehoiachin became king of Judah, he did evil in the sight of the Lord. The Lord sent Nebuchadnezzar, king of Babylon, against Judah. He laid siege to the city (2 Kings 24:10) and took Jehoiachin captive (2 Kings 24:12). He was brought to the land of Babylon, the land described here as the land of merchants and traders. King Jehoiachin seems to be the "top of the cedar" that the eagle (Nebuchadnezzar) planted in Babylon.

The eagle also took some seed from the land and planted it in fertile soil by an abundant source of water (verse 5). According to 2 Kings 24:16–17, Nebuchadnezzar made Zedekiah king in Judah in the place of Jehoiachin. He granted Zedekiah and his officials the right to govern the people who remained in the land of Judah. Anyone with ability had been taken by the Babylonians to serve as slaves in Babylon. Those who remained in Judah were the poor and unskilled. King Zedekiah was to rule over these individuals and assure their loyalty to the king of Babylon. King Zedekiah and those who remained in Israel may be the "seed" planted by the eagle in the fertile soil of Judah.

The seed the eagle planted grew into a vine and spread out its branches (verse 6). There was a certain growth under the leadership of Zedekiah. Note, however, that the branches reached out to the eagle. Zedekiah was committed to Nebuchadnezzar by an oath of faithfulness (see verse 13). He offered to him his submission and respect. Notice that while his "branches" reached out to Nebuchadnezzar, Zedekiah's "roots" remained firmly planted in the soil of Judah.

We now meet a second eagle (verse 7). This eagle was also great and powerful. Ezekiel tells us that, on seeing this second eagle, the vine bent its roots and branches and stretched them out toward this second bird. In doing so, the vine (Zedekiah and those who remained in Israel) turned away from the first eagle. Zedekiah was not only breaking an oath of faithfulness to Babylon but was also breaking the covenant relationship with God as well (verse 19). Notice here how the vine's roots would be pulled up (verse 9). Remember that these roots were planted in the soil of Israel, the land that God had promised. In turning from Nebuchadnezzar, they were also turning their backs on God, who had allowed them to remain in the promised land. We read in 2 Chronicles 36:13 concerning Zedekiah: "He also rebelled against King Nebuchadnezzar, who had made him take an oath in God's name. He became stiff-necked and hardened his heart and would not turn to the LORD, the God of Israel."

Zedekiah, having broken his treaty with Nebuchadnezzar, turned to the other "eagle" for help. Who was the second eagle? Jeremiah 37 tells us that, during the reign of Zedekiah, the Egyptians marched to the aid of Jerusalem (Jeremiah 37:5). Verse 15 confirms this. This second bird represented the nation of Egypt. As for Zedekiah, because he broke his covenant with the king of Babylon, verses 18–21 tell us that God would spread his net over him and bring him and his subjects to Babylon. The story of how this happened is recorded for us in Jeremiah 52. They refused to accept God's will for their lives and turned toward Egypt for help. They would not find the help they desired in Egypt. God's people would perish like this vine with its roots pulled up (verses 9–10). Like a dead vine, they would be gathered up and cast aside.

What is important for us to note here is that, while Babylon was the enemy of God's people, God expected Israel to submit to her for a time. Babylon was the nation that God would use to punish his people. In turning their backs on Babylon at this time, they were resisting the discipline of the Lord. We all know how hard the discipline of the Lord can be at times. Sometimes we just want it to stop. Sometimes we take things into our own hands to try to speed up the process. God calls us to accept his discipline. It is his means of making us the people he has called us to be. Instead of running from God, learn to trust and praise him for these times of discipline. He will use them for your good and his glory.

This was not the end of the story. God promised that he would take the top off another cedar and plant some young twigs from it on the top of a prominent mountain (verse 22). It would take root and become a splendid cedar. It would provide shelter for birds of every kind. This very clearly referred to the return of God's people to their own land. The entire world would see how God could take an insignificant people and make them into something great. There was hope for the people of God in spite of their rebellion. God had not finished with them.

What is the practical application of this chapter to our lives? Where has God planted you? What are your present circumstances? Zedekiah did not like where he had been planted. He did not like having to be subject to the king of Babylon. He could not accept that the Lord had allowed him to be planted in the soil of Babylonian domination. He chose to rebel against the will of the Lord. He broke his word to Babylon and reached out to the king of Egypt for help. He perished because he pulled up his roots from the soil in which God planted him.

What about you? Sometimes the will of God is very difficult. Sometimes we cannot understand why the Lord is allowing certain things to happen to us. It is better to let our roots sink deeply into the will of God, even when we do not understand, than to pull them up and take matters into our own hands. The temptation is to pull up our roots and abandon our post. Don't be like Zedekiah—keep your roots firmly planted in the will of God. Let nothing shake you. As long as your roots are planted in God, you will never perish. God will prove faithful in the end.

For Consideration:

- Why is the temptation so strong to abandon our post in times of trial? What causes us to become uneasy with God's will for our lives?

- Can God use what appears to be evil to accomplish good in our lives? What does this passage teach us about this?

- Can you recall a time when God used evil or tragedy in your life to accomplish great good? Explain.

For Prayer:

- Thank the Lord that he is a sovereign God who is able to transform even the most horrible tragedy into good in our lives.

- If you are going through a trial right now, ask the Lord to give you strength to wait upon him.

- Do you have a friend or acquaintance who is going through a hard time? Take a moment to ask the Lord to be with him or her through this trial.

18

The Sins of the Fathers

Read Ezekiel 18

There was a proverb in the land of Israel that went something like this: "The fathers have eaten sour grapes and the children's teeth are set on edge" (verse 2). What did it mean? It meant that children had to suffer because of the sins of their fathers. There is a certain truth in this statement. Speak to a child of an abusive father. Sit down with the child of an unfaithful or an alcoholic father. You will soon find out that what children experienced in the home very dramatically affects them in their lives today. In this sense the sins of the fathers have caused their children to suffer.

The children of Israel, however, took this a step further. They believed that when a father sinned, he acted for the entire family. They felt that God would punish the entire family because of the sins of the father. God told them here that this was not the case: "The soul who sins is the one who will die" (verse 4). Each individual is accountable to God for his or her own sins. We will never have to answer for the sins of another.

Ezekiel explains to us what he means by giving us four examples in this chapter. The first example is of a righteous father (verses 5–9). This father does not worship idols. He does not defile himself. He respects his neighbor's wife. He lives in harmony with those in his community. He shows compassion to the oppressed and provides for the needs of the poor. He observes the law of God. "This man," says God, "shall surely live" (verse 9 NKJV).

This righteous man, however, has a son (verses 10–13). His son is a violent man who worships idols. He oppresses the needy. He is unfaithful to his word. He is an adulterer. He takes advantage of his neighbor. "He," says the Lord, "shall surely die" (verse 13 NKJV). His righteous father will not be able to save him in the day of God's wrath. The fact that he was brought up in a godly home will not set him free from the wrath of God. He will perish for his sins, but his father will be saved. We cannot judge people on the basis of the family they come from or the church they attend. You can come from a good family and a good church and still be lost in your sins.

Ezekiel gives us a second example. Here he speaks about a son who recognizes the sins of his father and turns from them (verses 14–17). In this case the son would be saved and the father would perish. The son would not share the guilt of the father. The basic principle is found in verse 20: "The soul who sins is the one who will die. The son will not share the guilt of the father, nor will the father share the guilt of the son. The righteousness of the righteous man will be credited to him, and the wickedness of the wicked will be charged against him."

How easy it is for parents to blame themselves because their children have wandered from the path. The Bible tells us that each child is accountable to God for his or her own actions. You are not accountable to God for your children's sins. While we are accountable to God to bring up our children in the ways of the Lord, God does not hold us accountable for how they respond. They must answer to God for themselves.

Ezekiel gives us a third example in verses 21–23. Here we have the case of a sinful man who turns from his sins to serve the Lord. Ezekiel tells us that none of his past offenses will be remembered (verse 22). Think about this for a moment. Maybe you have come from a horrible background. You are ashamed of your past life. When you think about what you did before you met the Lord, it sends shivers down your spine. Looking at where you came from is depressing. Satan begins to plant seeds of doubt in your mind. You begin to wonder if the Lord could really forgive you. Ezekiel 18:22 tells us that "none of the offenses he has committed will be remembered against him." What does that small word *none* mean? Does it not mean *not one*? Not one of your offenses, not one sin (however small or however big) will be held against you if you are forgiven by the Lord God. What comfort you can take in this verse today. Bring those sins to him now. Confess them and surrender to God.

The final example is found in verse 24. Here we meet a righteous man who turns his back on the Lord. The Bible tells us that this man will die. In other words, he will be judged for his sin. Ezekiel reminds us that all his "righteousness which he has done shall not be remembered" (NKJV). He will not escape the judgment of God simply because he served the Lord faithfully in the past. Even believers have to give an account of their actions to the Lord (2 Corinthians 5:10).

Some people feel that God puts our sins on a scale and measures them against our good deeds. The teaching of Ezekiel here totally contradicts this idea. Sin is like a disease. When attacked by a disease, your previous good health is totally ignored. The disease cares nothing for all the physical exercise and nutritious food you ate in the past.

When this disease attacks you, it can take your life despite how healthy you have been all your life. So it is with sin. Our godly past does not guarantee that we will not fall prey to the disease of sin in the future. Sin can destroy a godly person as well as an ungodly person. It is no respecter of persons.

The people of Ezekiel's day could not accept this basic teaching (verses 25–29). They felt that God should at least take into consideration the fact that they were brought up in a good home. They believed that their righteous deeds should count for something, even though they were not living for God right then. There are many people who feel the same way today. They are trusting in their good deeds and good upbringing to get them through. God tells us here, however, that we will each give an individual account of our lives before God. Fathers will not answer for their children. Children cannot count on their parents. God will not measure our deeds on a scale. He wants to know where you are with him right now. Everything can be cleansed. You can be completely forgiven if you come to him—but you must come.

God pleads with his people to turn away from their sin. He longs to forgive them. He takes no pleasure in their death. It gives him great joy to bring life and healing to their souls. God offers them a new heart and spirit that is clean before him. He calls us to come to him and live. You alone can do something about your sins. No other person can help you.

For Consideration:

- What things do people count on today to get them to heaven?

- Is it possible for a righteous person to fall into sin? What areas of your life need to be guarded to protect you from falling today?

- Where do you stand with God today? Are you right with him? Explain.

For Prayer:

- Do you know people who are counting on their upbringing or church to get them to heaven? Take a moment to pray that God would reveal to them their need of the Savior.

- Do you have parents or children who have not yet come to the Lord? Ask God to bring them to himself.

- If you are a parent today, ask God to give you wisdom in the raising of your children. If you are not a parent, pray for a specific family you know.

19

The Lion and
the Vine

Read Ezekiel 19

Have you ever thought of where you would be today without God? Everything we have we owe to him. He pours his blessings so richly upon us. All too often, what God has given us we use for our own glory. We have become proud and arrogant. We have boasted that we are self-made people. We turn our backs on God. This was the case for Israel and her kings. Israel needed to learn that the God who blessed could also remove his blessings. In this chapter we meet two kings of Israel. They are depicted as great lions. Because they misused the glory the Lord had given them and arrogantly turned their backs on God, he would remove them from power. In this section Israel is also compared to a beautiful vine that God uprooted because of her rebellious heart. Let's look at these illustrations.

Israel was a lioness bringing up her cubs. One cub, in particular, became very strong and powerful. He grew up to become a magnificent lion. He was a lion to be feared. He tore apart his prey and devoured men. Because he was such an evil and fearful lion, a trap was set for him. Men dug a pit to ensnare him. He fell into their trap. His captors led him away to Egypt where he would no longer be a threat to them.

To whom is this illustration referring? Many commentators believe that this lion is King Jehoahaz. Israel, as the lioness, gave birth to this great king. He was a bad king. The Bible tells us about Jehoahaz: "He did evil in the eyes of the LORD, just as his fathers had done" (2 Kings 23:32). Three months into his reign, Pharaoh Neco put him in chains and led him away into captivity in Egypt (see 2 Kings 23:31–33). Jehoahaz, like the lion, was trapped and sent into exile in the land of Egypt.

With her first lion cub gone, Israel, the lioness, was forced to turn her attention to another cub. She raised a second cub to replace the first. This cub was the same as his brother. He tore apart his prey. He devoured men. He ravaged towns. People were terrified of his roaring. The nations assembled against him. They captured him and led him away into captivity in Babylon.

Who is this second lion? Pharaoh placed Jehoahaz's brother Eliakim on the throne. According to 2 Kings 23:34, Pharaoh changed the name of Eliakim to Jehoiakim. Jehoiakim proved to be an evil king like his brother. In 2 Kings 24:2 we read that, because of his evil ways, God sent many nations against him. We have a record in this verse of the nations of Babylon, Aram (Syria), Moab, and Ammon all attacking Israel at this time. This corresponds perfectly with Ezekiel 19:8.

During the reign of Jehoiakim, Nebuchadnezzar invaded the land and forced Jehoiakim to become his servant. For three years Jehoiakim served the king of Babylon. After three years, however, he rebelled against Babylon (see 2 Kings 24:1). This caused the Babylonians to invade Judah, the southern kingdom of Israel. According to 2 Chronicles 36:5–7, Jehoiakim was bound with bronze shackles and led off into captivity to Babylon. This second lion cub was treated in the same way as the first. He was removed from his position and taken into captivity. All these things happened just as God had prophesied through his servant Ezekiel.

The second picture here in this chapter is the picture of a vine. For the third time in the book of Ezekiel, the people of God are compared to a vine (see chapters 15 and 17). As a vine, Israel was planted by the waters. Because of her ideal location, she brought forth much fruit. Her branches were strong and beautiful. Her foliage was thick. She grew tall. Her branches were fit to make a ruler's scepter.

This vine, however, was uprooted. She was thrown to the ground. Her fruit was stripped from her. The east wind came and shrivelled her up. Her branches withered and she was consumed by fire. She was replanted in the desert. What a sorry sight she was then. She was fruitless, sickly, and withered. Her branches, once fit to make a ruler's scepter, were no longer of any use.

Babylon was the east wind that came and withered the vine of God's people. When the Babylonians came, they stripped Judah of her possessions. They burned her houses and temple. They took the shrivelled up vine and exiled her into Babylon, where she was replanted. There in exile all pride and dignity were removed. She was a sickly people of no use to God.

God's people, like her kings, had turned their backs on him. They had been a great nation. At one point they were feared by the surrounding nations. Israel was like the great lion whose roar sent fear into the hearts of those who heard it. They were a prosperous people. They flourished under the blessings of God. Israel was like the vine whose branches were fit to make a ruler's scepter. But God's people became proud and arrogant. They felt they did not need God. They felt they could take care of themselves. Because of their rebellion, the Lord God took away his blessings. They were stripped of all his favor. They withered up and became the laughingstock of all the nations.

Where would we be today without God? If you serve the Lord in some ministry, where would that ministry be without the Lord? Consider for a moment the many blessings you have. From whose hand have you received these blessings? Who makes your heart beat? Who gives you each breath you breathe? Who gives you life and strength? Without the Lord you would perish.

Let's learn the lesson of this chapter. How quickly God could remove his presence from our ministries. How quickly he could withdraw the blessings he has poured out on us. How much we owe our great God. Let's not take him for granted. The great lions of Israel were captured. The great vine of Israel was uprooted. It could happen to us as well, were it not for the grace and mercy of a loving God. Praise him for all he has done for you. Use the blessings he has given you to serve and honor him in return. Do not take his blessings for granted. How quickly he could remove what he has given to us!

For Consideration:

- Consider for a moment some of the blessings God has given to you in recent years. Would any of this be possible without him?

- Why is it so hard to admit that without God we would have nothing?

- What would it take for everything you have worked so hard to achieve in life to be taken from you?

- Have you ever found yourself looking at your achievements and thinking, even for a moment, that you were the one who accomplished these things? What do you learn from this chapter?

For Prayer:

- Thank God for the evidence of his blessing in your life today.

- Ask him to forgive you for the times you failed to recognize his hand in your life.

- Ask him to help you use these blessings for his glory.

20

Rebellion Broken

Read Ezekiel 20

Have you ever met a person who accepted the Lord but wandered away from him? These people are all too common in our day. Maybe the wanderer is someone close to you. Maybe it is a son or a daughter. Maybe your husband or wife has lost his or her first love for the Lord Jesus. Could it be you? God's people in Ezekiel's day were in this situation.

As we begin this chapter, the elders of the land had come to the prophet Ezekiel to inquire of the Lord. They recognized his gift, but they were unwilling to listen to what he said. This was not the first time in this book that they had come to inquire of the Lord. They had come in chapter 14 to hear the Word of the Lord. Notice here in verse 3 what the Lord had to say to them: "Son of man, speak to the elders of Israel and say to them, 'This is what the Sovereign Lord says: Have you come to inquire of me? As surely as I live, I will not let you inquire of me, declares the Sovereign Lord.'"

Why would the Lord not want to speak to these elders? To answer this question, God took them back to the time of their forefathers. He reminded them of how he had revealed himself to them in the land of Egypt. They had been crying out to him in their bondage and oppression. God heard their cry and came to them through his servant Moses. He searched out for them a land of milk and honey and placed them in a most beautiful land. In return for his great favor, he simply asked them to turn from their idols to serve him. They refused to put aside these idols, however. Instead, they continued to worship the gods of Egypt. God wanted to pour out his anger on them. Instead, however, he chose to exercise patience (verse 9). Why did he choose not to destroy them? "But for the sake of my name I did what would keep it from being profaned in the eyes of the nations they lived among and in whose sight I had revealed myself to the Israelites by bringing them out of Egypt" (verse 9).

God chose not to "profane" (NIV) or "pollute" (KJV) his name in the sight of the nations. What would the nations say if the people of God were destroyed? Would they not blaspheme his name? "What kind of God is this who would destroy his people?" they would ask. He exercised patience so that all would see his great love and patience toward his people.

Despite their sin, the Lord led his people out of the land of Egypt. He gave them his laws to distinguish them from all the other people of the earth. He warned them that they would disobey these laws at the cost of their own lives. God called them to set aside one day in seven as a day of rest and fellowship with him. Once again, however, his people refused to obey. They rejected and despised his laws. They defiled the holy day the Lord gave them. Again, the Lord thought of destroying them for their sins, but again he withheld his hand. What kept him from judging them? "But for the sake of my name I did what would keep it from being profaned in the eyes of the nations in whose sight I had brought them out" (verse 14).

Once again, we see that for the sake of his name, God chose to exercise patience and compassion on these sinners. While that generation would perish in the wilderness because of their sin, the nation was not destroyed. God's grace and compassion would again be showered on their children.

God spoke to these children. He commanded them to keep his commandments and not follow the ways of their parents. They had the advantage of seeing the judgment of God on their parents in the wilderness. These children, like their parents, however, chose to turn their backs on God (verse 21). They did not obey his laws. For the third time in this chapter, we read that the Lord wanted to destroy them as a people. He withheld his hand, however. Again, verse 22 gives us the reason: "But I withheld my hand, and for the sake of my name I did what would keep it from being profaned in the eyes of the nations in whose sight I had brought them out."

Once again, for the sake of his name, the Lord chose not to destroy his people. They would not go unpunished, however. God would scatter them to the ends of the earth (verse 23). He also gave them up to their evil practices (verse 25). Because of their sinful ways, God declared their worship of him to be unclean. Notice here how their gifts and offerings were mere rituals (verse 26). On the one hand, they offered their gifts to the Lord; and on the other hand, they made their firstborn children pass through the fire in honor of their pagan gods (verse 26). Not only did they do this, but verse 28 tells us that they went up into the high mountains and hills and offered sacrifices and offerings to the gods of the land. They forsook the one true God who delivered them from the land of Egypt. These places where they worshiped their foreign gods, God called *bamah*, meaning "high place." The children did exactly as their parents had done. They had completely defiled themselves before God. Verse 32 tells us that their desire was to be like the Gentile nations around them. They wanted to serve their gods and bow down to their idols. They had made up their minds. They did not want the God of their fathers.

How would God respond toward this people? He responded not in the way they deserved, not even in a way we would expect. "What you have in mind will never happen," said the Lord (verse 32). God would not allow them to continue in their rebellion: "I will rule over you," (verse 33).

Yes, God would rule over them even in their rebellion. He would gather them from the far corners of the earth where they had wandered. He would plead with them face to face (verse 35). He would count them like a shepherd counted his sheep, as they passed under his rod. As they passed under this rod, he would purge them. The rebels among them would be disciplined. In that day, God's people would see a great working of his Spirit in their midst.

When he had purged them, they would again serve their God. Once again, God would be pleased to accept their willing, heartfelt offerings and sacrifices. He would sanctify them in the eyes of the nations around them. Everyone would know that Israel belonged to God. The nations would see God's hand print all over his people. As God's Spirit moved among them, they would remember their evil ways and how they had rebelled against the Lord. They would loathe themselves because of their evil. They would be brought to repentance. In all this they would see his wonderful grace toward them.

In verse 46 God told Ezekiel to turn toward the south and prophesy against it. Ezekiel was in Babylon. As he looked toward the south, he looked toward the land God had given to the Jews. He told the elders that the Lord had started a fire in the land that would not be quenched. The land would be destroyed. God was going to begin his purging of the land. That purging would take place through the nation of Babylon, which would invade and conquer their land. The elders of the land who had come to see Ezekiel were not able to understand what God was saying through his prophet. To them, he was speaking in parables with hidden meanings. They could not understand what was wrong. Why was God angry? What had they done that would deserve such wrath? As spiritual and political leaders, they were totally blind to the things of God.

What is the application of this passage to us in our present day? Do we not have here a great encouragement regarding our loved ones who have wandered from their initial commitment to the Lord? God refused here to destroy his people for the sake of his name. When we accept the Lord as our Savior, we become his children and take his name upon ourselves. God's desire in this chapter was to preserve those who were called by his name. In spite of their sins, they were kept. While they were punished, they were never abandoned. God would not allow his people to continue in their rebellion. They would be purged. The evil would be removed, and they would return to him with faithful hearts. God is still sovereign in the lives of those who rebel against him.

Do you have loved ones who have forsaken their first love of the Lord? Can we not claim this chapter for these loved ones? Can we not claim the promise of God that he will purge those who are his, even though they have wandered from him? What about your son or daughter? What about your husband or wife? If God refused to abandon his people in the Old Testament because of his name sake, will he not be as faithful to his children today? If God promised that he would purge his people in the days of Ezekiel, can we not claim this promise for our friends and loved ones who have wandered from the path of truth today? Will God abandon

his child today when he refused to do so in Ezekiel's day?
Friends, take courage. The God who ruled over his rebellious
children (verse 33) and brought them back to the fold in the
days of Ezekiel is the same God today. Do not lose heart. He
will not forsake his own.

For Consideration:

- Have you ever had a time of wandering from the Lord? In
  all that time did God ever abandon you?

- What courage do you take from this chapter with regard to
  our nation and the church of our day?

- Take a moment to consider how the Lord has exercised
  patience toward you over the last few years.

For Prayer:

- Thank the Lord for his patience toward you today.

- Do you know some people who are presently wandering
  from the Lord? Take a moment to ask the Lord to work in
  their lives, even as he promised here to work in the lives of
  his people in Israel.

21

A Sword Sharpened and Polished

Read Ezekiel 21

We saw in the last chapter how God promised to pour out a spirit of repentance on his people (Ezekiel 20:43). While he could have destroyed them, his love and mercy preserved them. God is a God of enormous love and compassion. He is also, however, a God of righteous anger and judgment. Here in this chapter God reminds his people that a day of judgment is coming.

The prophet was called on to prophesy against the holy places in the city of Jerusalem. Notice here that it was not against the dens of iniquity that he was to preach. He was to speak out against the holy places. It was here that God should have been worshiped. Here the name of the Almighty should have been lifted up, but instead it was being dishonored.

Verse 3 tells us that the Lord was against these holy places. He was, even then, drawing his sword from its sheath to cut them off (kill them). Notice here that he was going to cut off "both the righteous and the wicked." From the north to the south, all flesh would experience the heavy hand of God's wrath. Why would the righteous have to suffer along with the wicked? Could it be that the righteous too had drifted far from God? Had they become complacent in their day? Had they become indifferent to the evils around them? Were they being tempted to follow the ways of the world? What is clear here is that everyone was to be placed under the stern hand of God's judgment. The righteous needed to be awakened from their sleep of indifference.

God called the prophet to groan before the people with a broken heart (verse 6). We are not told here how the prophet did this. It is clear from the context, however, that he did so in a way that drew attention to himself. When the people asked him why he was grieving so deeply, he was to tell them that it was because of what the Lord God had planned to do to them. We should understand here that Ezekiel very likely felt this grief in his heart. The heart of the prophet literally felt the pain and anguish of God. Ezekiel would have to act this out. Very likely God would have burdened his heart over the judgment that was coming on his people. Maybe he needs to burden our hearts in a similar way.

Ezekiel reminded the people that the day was coming when every heart would melt. Their hands would go limp. Their spirits would become faint. Their knees would become weak because of the severity of the Lord's wrath. As we consider our own lives before God, where do we stand? We will all one day stand before this great judge. Will we be ready? What is our response to the declining spiritual condition of our land? Have our hearts been broken like Ezekiel's? Have we groaned with great grief? Are we aware of the judgment that is soon coming?

The sword of the Lord was against his people. It was being sharpened and polished for slaughter. It would flash among them with the speed and devastation of lightning.

This was not a time to be joyous. No resistance was possible. Even the king's scepter and all it represented would not be able to resist the sword of God's wrath. Like iron against wood, the judgment of the Lord would come smashing down on them (see verse 21). Even as God was speaking to Ezekiel, that sword was being polished and sharpened. It would soon be handed over to the slayer who would execute God's sentence on the earth.

This was a time to cry and wail (verse 12). God asked Ezekiel to beat his breast (strike his thigh, NKJV) as a sign of mourning. Terror was about to fall on the people of God and against the princes of the land. God's sword would not overlook the scepter (symbol of the king of Judah). He too would have to suffer the consequences of his rebellion against God. He would not be able to resist God in this matter.

In verse 14 Ezekiel reminded the people that this sword of God's judgment would do tremendous damage in the land. It would enter into the private chambers (NKJV) of the land and deal with the sin of the hidden places. There would be nowhere to hide. The sword would await them at all the gates to the city. The picture here was fugitives seeking to escape the city under judgment. As they fled the enemy waited for them at the gate, cutting them down one by one. Panic would strike. Verse 16 speaks of a great sword swinging to the left and to the right, devouring everything in its path. God's anger would not subside until he had executed his full judgment on the land (verse 17).

How would this sword of God's judgment come on the people of God? It would come by means of the nation of Babylon. God told Ezekiel to make a signpost (verse 19). This sign would point in two directions. The first direction was toward the town of Rabbah in the land of Ammon. The second direction was toward the city of Jerusalem in Judah. God was going to judge these two nations.

The king of Babylon was seen standing in the fork of the road, examining the signpost made by Ezekiel (verse 21). Where would he send his army first? He would cast lots to decide. Some commentators believe that he wrote the names of the cities on arrows in his quiver, and then drew one of these arrows out of his quiver. The city whose name was written on the first arrow he drew from his quiver would be the city he would attack first. He would consult his idols before making a choice. He would examine the liver (obviously a pagan ritual for determining the will of the gods). Jerusalem would be chosen first. She would be destroyed. While we see the king of Babylon consulting his idols, it was really the Lord God who determined the king's course. God was sovereign even over these evil practices.

Verse 23 tells us that those who had sworn allegiance to Babylon (the king of Judah and his princes) would not believe that their nation would be destroyed. They believed that they were safe and secure. God, however, was going to surprise them by judging their sin. There are many people like this in our day. Somehow they believe that they are safe from the judgment of God. The day will come when they will have to stand before God to give an account of their actions. What a terrible day that will be.

Because they had openly rebelled against God, they would be "taken in hand" (NKJV) or "taken captive" (verse 24). Their day had come. "Remove the crown," God said to the princes of the land. This was a day for humbling. God gave permission to the Babylonians to overthrow his people. They would not be restored until the day that God handed the nation over to the one to whom it rightfully belonged (verse 27). Who was the one to whom the nation rightfully belonged? Is it not the Lord Jesus, the Messiah? He alone would be able to set their hearts right. He alone would be able to restore them to the Lord their God. He alone was their hope. Notice here how powerless the people of God really were. They fell prey to the enemy. They were being trampled on and oppressed. Ultimately, they had only themselves to blame. They had turned from their God—now they would suffer the deadly consequences of their rebellion and sin.

As for the nation of Ammon, the other name on the signpost, it would not be forgotten. There was an arrow with her name on it as well. They were not to trust the false visions of their prophets who were only deceiving them. What were these prophets telling them? Were they telling them that everything would be all right? How often have we heard that message in our day? They were announcing peace when there was no peace. God would pour out his wrath upon them as well (verse 31). They would be handed over to men skilled in destruction (verse 31). They would become fuel for the fire of God's wrath. Their blood would be shed, and they would be remembered no more (verse 32).

Notice here that the first to be judged were the people of God. They knew better. They had received the law of God and knew his ways but rejected him. They were his children, the objects of his very special attention. When they rebelled against him, they experienced the heavy hand of his judgment. Their judgment was not pleasant. It was not expected, though it was clearly prophesied. They did not believe that God would ever discipline them the way he did. Maybe we too can feel this way. We know that God does not like the sins in our lives, but we feel that his patience will last forever. What a surprise it was for the Israelites to wake one day to the realization that now they were going to have to answer to God for their sin. While the patience of God is very real, so is his judgment. Let's not tempt him. Instead, learn the lesson of this chapter. Deal with your sins. Confess them and be made right with God. Don't put it off. One day it will be too late.

For Consideration:

- Consider for a moment the condition of the church of our day. What keeps God from judging today?

- What do we cling to today for security? What makes us feel that God will never really call us to give an account of our sins?

- How do we find the balance between teaching that God is love and also that he is a God of justice and wrath? Do you find a balance in this teaching in your church? How important is this balance?

For Prayer:

- Ask God to reach out to the church of our day and renew it. Ask him to send a revival to awaken his church before it is too late.

- Take a moment to look deeply into your own heart. If the sword of the Lord were to enter your "private chamber" what would it find?

- Thank God for the incredible patience he has demonstrated toward you in your failures and shortcomings.

22

Standing in the Gap

Read Ezekiel 22

God was very angry with his people. In the last meditation we saw how he had been polishing and sharpening his sword to do battle with his people. God's anger was not without reason. In Ezekiel 22 he accused his people of twenty-nine transgressions of his Word. In verse 1 the prophet Ezekiel was called to stand as judge. As he listened, God brought his accusations against the people. God accused his people of the following sins:

1. Shedding innocent blood (verses 3–4)
2. Idolatry (verses 3–4)
3. Misuse of the prince's power to shed blood (verse 6)
4. Treating their fathers and mothers with contempt (verse 7)
5. Oppression of the foreigner (verse 7)
6. Mistreatment of the orphan (verse 7)
7. Mistreatment of the widow (verse 7)

8. Despising the holy things of God (verse 8)
9. Profaning the Sabbath (verse 8)
10. Slander (verse 9)
11. Committing lewd acts on the mountaintops of Israel (verse 9)
12. Eating at the pagan mountain shrines (verse 9)
13. Having sexual intercourse with their mothers (verse 10)
14. Violation of women during their impurity (verse 10)
15. Violation of their neighbors' wives (verse 11)
16. Violation of their daughters-in law (verse 11)
17. Violation of their sisters (verse 11)
18. Accepting bribes to shed blood (verse 12)
19. Taking [charging] excessive interest (verse 12)
20. Taking advantage of their neighbors by extortion (verse 12)
21. Forsaking the Lord (verse 12)
22. The princes (NIV) or prophets (NKJV) devouring the people (verse 25)
23. The priests doing violence to the law (verse 26)
24. The officials (NIV) or princes (NKJV) murdering the people for gain (verse 27)
25. The prophets speaking lies in God's name (verse 28)
26. Extortion (NIV) or oppression (NKJV, verse 29)
27. Robbery (verse 29)
28. Mistreating the poor (verse 29)
29. Oppressing the foreigner (verse 29)

God was rightfully angered against his people. Their unrestrained sin caused the day of their judgment to draw near (verse 4). Notice here that our sin and rebellion against God can actually hasten his judgment. There comes a point where our sin is so great that God must pour out his judgment on our land. Already God's people were seeing the results of their sin. God had made them to be a laughingstock in the eyes of the nations. The surrounding nations despised them. They no longer had the favor of God on them, nor did they have the favor of the nations around them. Their former glory had all but disappeared (verse 5).

God beat his fists in anger because of the dishonesty and sin of his people (verse 13 NKJV). There was frustration in his voice as he cried out: "What will happen in the day that I deal with you? Will your heart and hands be strong on that day?" (verse 14). Because of their sin, the people of God would be scattered among the nations (verse 15). Just as metal was refined in the furnace, so God's people would be cast into the furnace of his discipline and wrath. There, under his mighty justice, their resistance would be melted. As a people they refused the refreshing rain of God's renewal (verse 24). The day was coming, however, when they would again recognize him as Lord and turn to him (see verses 17–22). We have seen evidence of this throughout the history of God's people. We read of the revival that took place under Josiah in 2 Kings 23 when God's people recommitted themselves to the covenant he had given them. This resulted in the temple being cleansed of its impurities and the idols of the land being torn down. We also see in the days of Ezra and Nehemiah another great move of God among his people (see Nehemiah 8). Here Ezra read the Word of God from daybreak until noon, while the priests explained its meaning. This resulted in the people falling on their faces to the ground, weeping with the realization that they had fallen short of God's standard. While there have been times of refreshing for God's people, the Jews, it seems to me that God still has a wonderful plan to reach out to them in a very special way.

When God looked on his people, he looked for even one person in whom he could find favor so he wouldn't have to destroy them. But he could not find that one individual among them. They were completely sold out to sin, from the least to the greatest. Because of this, God would shower his righteous anger on them. The fire of his wrath would consume them. God would repay them for their evil deeds. It is true that Ezekiel had been faithful to the Lord, but among all the people of the land there was no one else who sought after the Lord.

We are left to believe here that even one righteous person among them could have preserved the nation. This reminds us of the cities of Sodom and Gomorrah. God told Abraham that if he could even find ten righteous people in these cities, he would spare them. This appears to be the case here. Our influence has a preserving effect in our society. Jesus calls us the "salt of the earth" (Matthew 5:13). There are times when the only thing that keeps God from unleashing his wrath on this world is his love for his children. What an important role we play.

Could it be that God is calling you to stand in the gap for someone today? In chapter 21 we saw that the sword of God's judgment was being sharpened. It was ready to fall. God took no delight in condemning his people. He grieved because no one approached him to seek his mercy on behalf of his people. How quickly he would have forgiven them, but no one sought that forgiveness. In Exodus 32:9–14 God told Moses that he was going to destroy his people because of their sin. Moses stood in the gap and pleaded for Israel. God willingly spared them because of Moses' prayer. Is God calling you to stand in the gap for your friends today? Does God want you to seek his face on their behalf? Perhaps his sword of judgment is dangling over their heads right now. Perhaps only your prayers will keep it from falling.

How does our own nation measure up to the nation of Judah? Take the time to reexamine the twenty-nine complaints of God against his people. Isn't our nation as guilty of sin as the nation of Judah? When God looks down on our land, can he find a man or a woman who will go against flow? Will you be that man or woman who stands in the gap? Praise God for those who stand firm for the truth. Could it be that they are the reason that the judgment of God is withheld for a time? May we be faithful. By our faithfulness to the Word of God, we may yet save our nation from the judgment of God.

For Consideration:

- Compare the sins of Israel with what is happening in your nation today. How does your nation measure up?

- Is there someone for whom you need to stand in the gap today?

- What does this chapter teach us about God's desire to forgive?

- How does the Lord Jesus stand in the gap for us?

For Prayer:

- Pray for your nation. Ask God to spare it from his judgment.

- Do you know someone who has wandered from God? Ask God for mercy on behalf of that person.

23

Oholah and Oholibah

Read Ezekiel 23

They say that history repeats itself. We never seem to learn from the mistakes of others. As parents we speak to our children about the dangers of certain actions. It seems, however, that our children are bound to repeat our mistakes. Experience is really the best teacher. We never understand what our parents taught us until we experience these things ourselves. How unfortunate this is. How much better the world would be if we could only learn from the experience of others. In this chapter we meet two young women by the names of Oholah and Oholibah. These young women were sisters. They represented the cities of Samaria and Jerusalem and seemed to be destined to learn their lessons the hard way.

Oholah was the older sister (verse 4) She represented Samaria, the capital of the northern kingdom of Israel (verse 4). Oholah grew up in Egypt (verse 3). Here, under the leadership of Moses, she had her birth as a nation. Oholah had a rebellious heart. She became a prostitute very early in life. She lusted after other gods. There in Egypt she turned away from God to serve the idols of the Egyptians. Though she belonged to God and had given him many sons and daughters (verse 4), she is pictured in verse 3 as having her breasts fondled and her bosom caressed by foreigners. In other words, she turned to and courted the world instead of being faithful to her God.

When God set her free from Egypt under Moses, she lusted after the gods of the other nations (verse 5). These nations, with all their luxuries, attracted her. She was enticed by their rich clothing and desirable young men on horseback. She also defiled herself with the idols of the nation of Assyria (verse 7). In other words, she served other gods and turned her back on the God of Israel.

From a very early age Oholah had turned her back on her true husband. All through her youth she had been guilty of defiling herself with other gods. What began in Egypt continued throughout her life as a nation. As a jealous husband, God was angry. He gave Oholah over to her Assyrian lovers (verse 9). They stripped her naked, took away all she possessed, destroyed her land, stole her possessions, and killed her sons and daughters. In the end they killed Oholah. She was destroyed by the very one she lusted after.

Be assured that Satan will continue to entice us in this way today. He will make sin look attractive. He pretends to be "an angel of light" (2 Corinthians 11:14). By deception he will lead us straight into his trap. When we fall prey to his temptations, we find ourselves engulfed and destroyed by the very things that attracted us. This is what happened to Oholah (Israel). She sought after the gods of the nations. Ultimately, this was what destroyed her.

It is important that we notice here that God gave up Oholah to the ones she lusted after. While there is no temptation too much for us to overcome in God's strength, if we persist in our desire for evil, he may very well give us over to those desires. Lust, greed, bitterness, anger, and many other such evils can overcome the believer as well as the unbeliever. How many of us have been defeated by one or more of these enemies?

Oholah's sister, Oholibah, was very much like her. She represented the city of Jerusalem, capital of the southern kingdom of Israel (Judah). She too grew up in the land of Egypt. Like her sister, she too became a prostitute in the land of Egypt. When she left Egypt under Moses, like her sister, she lusted after the Assyrians and their gods.

Oholibah saw what happened to her sister (verse 11). Judah watched the Assyrians take the northern kingdom of Israel into captivity for her sin. She saw the end result of her sister's spiritual prostitution. Despite what she saw, she did not learn her lesson. She repeated the sins of her sister. She not only lusted after the Assyrians and their gods but also after the Babylonians and their gods as well (verse 14).

Notice the progression here in verses 14–17. Oholibah began by looking at the pictures of these Babylonian men portrayed with their flowing turbans and richly adorned belts. She allowed herself to focus on them. As she looked at these pictures, she began to lust after them (verse 17). Having allowed herself to lust after them, she proceeded to the next stage; she sent messengers to them in Babylon. Notice that she did not have the courage to go to them herself. Seeing her interest in them, the Babylonians came to her. She did not have to go to them. Be assured that if Satan knows you are interested and have entertained lustful thoughts in your heart, he will send temptation your way. All this led her to committing adultery with the Babylonians (verse 17) and eventually to open prostitution and rebellion against God. This first act led to further acts. In verse 19 she is said to be guilty of multiplying her immoral acts. Her immorality ultimately drove God from her presence (verse 18).

How often have individuals become trapped in an immoral lifestyle by the same process? Like the people of Judah, they allowed themselves to look at the pornography around them. These pictures caused them to lust. Their lust, in turn, drove them to immorality. Judah became more and more comfortable with the sin around her. We need to be aware so we don't also fall into the same trap. How important it is for us to nip lust in the bud.

Because of her sin, God, her husband, turned away from her in disgust. Despite the fact that her actions had separated her from God, she refused to stop what she was doing. Instead, she gave herself even more fully to her sin. Verse 20 is somewhat difficult to understand. Her lovers are described as having "flesh" like a donkey and "issue" like a horse (NKJV). The NIV translates it this way: "Whose genitals were like those of donkeys and whose emission was like that of horses." The idea here seems to be that their sexual appetite could not be satisfied. Her lovers had become slaves to their flesh. This was now the company that she kept. How different they were from God, her gentle and loving husband.

God stirred up Oholibah's lovers against her (verse 22). Those young men she desired would come to her. They would not come, however, to satisfy her lust—they would come to destroy her (verse 24). They would come to her with weapons in hand (verse 24). She would be punished for her sin. Her sons and daughters would be taken away (verse 25). She would be stripped of her possessions (verse 26). Everything she had worked for would be taken away from her (verse 29). She would be exposed for who she really was (verse 29). Oholibah would drink the same cup as her sister (verse 32). It was a cup of sorrow, desolation, and pain (verse 33). She would bear the consequences of her sin (verse 35). If only she had learned from her sister's experience. How often, like Oholibah, have we too been tempted by sin? It appears so attractive. Our lust overcomes us. When we finally give in to our lust, we find that it was not at all what we expected. Instead of satisfying us, these sins leave us empty, aching, guilty, ashamed, and dying.

God asked Ezekiel to confront the nation of Judah with her sin. She had committed adultery (verse 37). She had sacrificed her children to idols (verse 37). In other words, she had practiced the evil pagan rite of child sacrifice, offering her very own children on the altars of the pagan gods. She had defiled the sanctuary of God and his Sabbath (verse 38). She would practice child sacrifice and then come to the temple to call on God on the same day (verse 39). She lusted after the nations around her (verses 40–45). Even in her old age, she continued to rebel against the Almighty (verses 43–44). God called upon an angry mob to stone her for her adultery. He would make her an example for others. He would not allow her evil to continue (verse 48). Ultimately, she would know that God was the one true God.

How easy it is to fall into the trap of sin like Israel and Judah. How easy it is to turn our attention to the things of the world. We are often tempted to lust after earthly pleasures. How strongly we feel the pull to turn our eyes away from our God. We often look to other sources of help in our times of fear and crisis. It is not only those who are ignorant of the Word of God who turn their backs on him. The lure of sin is often stronger than our desire to be obedient. For the pleasure of sin, we willingly disobey. God was angry with Oholibah because she repeated the sins of her evil sister. She had seen how God had punished Oholah for her sins but refused to learn her lesson. Her punishment would be more severe. God warns us here of the dangers of turning our backs on him and repeating the errors of Israel and Judah. Will we be like Oholibah and block our ears? Will we learn from her experience, or are we doomed to fall ourselves into the same sin?

The example of Oholah and Oholibah is here for our reflection. May we reexamine our own lives. Are we right with our Lord? Have we, like these two sisters, turned our backs on God to seek after something else? Is the history of Oholah and Oholibah bound to repeat itself in your life? May God cause us to think long and hard about this example so we don't fall into the same trap.

For Consideration:

- What do we learn from this section about the dangers of pornography?

- Have you ever been in a situation where you repeated the error of someone else? What motivated you to ignore the example of those around you?

- What does this section teach us about the importance of dealing with sin?

For Prayer:

- Are you struggling with a particular attraction to sin?

- Ask God to show you what he would have you take from this chapter?

- Ask him to forgive you for the times you fell prey to the temptations of the enemy.

- Thank the Lord for the many warnings he has given us in his Word.

24

The Parable of the Cooking Pot

Read Ezekiel 24:1–14

Have you ever burned a pot dry? This can be a very frustrating experience. What makes this experience even more disheartening is when that pot contains the choice meat you so carefully selected at the market. Chapter 24 of Ezekiel presents a powerful illustration of a cooking pot boiled dry. Notice in verse 2 that the day God gave this parable to Ezekiel was the day the King of Babylon started his siege of Jerusalem. This parable, then, related to the siege of Jerusalem by Babylon.

God often used object lessons to teach the people of Israel about their sin. The cooking pot in this chapter was filled with water and put on the fire. The choicest pieces of meat were placed inside. Wood was piled up under the pot for a fire. The water was brought to a boil. The meat remained simmering in the boiling water (verse 5).

God's people, like this pot, had been placed over the fire of God's discipline. God delighted in his people like a cook rejoiced over a choice cut of meat. The fire of God's discipline under them was intended to bring out the best in them. Like a master chef, God placed just the right spices in the pot with the meat (verse 10). With time and patience, God's people would become everything the master cook intended them to become.

God's discipline, though for our good, is never easy. There are times when we rebel against God and what he wants to do in our lives. As a master cook, however, God is carefully preparing us. He takes great delight in us. As we allow him to work, he makes us into an object of beauty. The heat removes all the raw sin in our lives. The spices give us a flavor that is pleasing to him. Unlike earthly cooks, this cook never fails in his attempts. We can trust him fully.

Notice in this parable that there was a scum found in this boiling pot. This scum could not be removed despite the intense heat (verse 6). God had disciplined his children, but they would not listen to him. Sin, like this scum, tarnished their lives. They clung to their sin. They refused to let the natural process of cooking purify them.

According to verse 7, God's people were unashamed of their evil. Ezekiel said that they poured out on a rock the blood of innocent people. Blood poured out on a rock would be there for everyone to see. Jerusalem made no effort to conceal her evil. She felt no need to shed her innocent blood on the ground where it could be hidden and covered by the dust. She openly sinned against her God. Because she openly sinned against God, she would be openly punished. God would shed her blood on the rock where everyone would see it (verse 8).

Jerusalem was like this cooking pot. Inside the pot was the choicest of meat. God's people were like that choice meat. They turned away from God and left the scum of their sin caked on the side of the pot. The whole city was filled with their sin. Because they had refused God's gentle discipline, they would be punished more severely. Wood was heaped up under the cooking pot. The scum of Jerusalem's sins would be burned out by an even greater heat and removed, one piece at a time (verse 6). The meat itself (symbol of God's people) would be consumed. This would happen when the Babylonians invaded and destroyed their land.

Notice in verse 11 that the empty, over-boiled pot would then be taken and placed directly in the coals. It would be left in these coals until its copper began to glow with the heat. All its impurities would be destroyed. This pot represented the city of Jerusalem. It would be plundered and burned when Babylon invaded.

What was so unfortunate about this whole situation was the fact that both the meat and the pot had to be consumed. If the people of God had learned to accept his discipline on a daily basis, they would not have had to suffer the way they did. The more sin they heaped up in their lives, the more fire was necessary to consume that sin. Had they learned to heed the gentle heat of God's discipline, they would not have had to suffer the blazing fury of his judgment.

Some of us, like the children of Israel, have never learned to accept the gentle discipline of the Lord. We fail to listen to his exhortation in small matters. We do not deal with the small sins he speaks to us about. Do not heap up your sins like the people of Israel and Judah. Let the gentle heat of God's discipline cleanse you of your sins, or soon the only thing that will cleanse you will be the blazing heat of his judgment.

For Consideration:

• Why is it so hard for us to admit our sin and accept the gentle discipline of the Lord?

- How do you recognize the discipline of the Lord?

- Are there things in your life that you need to deal with today? What are they?

- How does the discipline of God tell us that he loves us?

For Prayer:

- Ask God to help you recognize his gentle discipline in your life.

- Thank him that you can trust what he is doing in your life even when it seems difficult.

- Thank him that he loves you enough to discipline and correct you when you are wrong.

25
The Death of Ezekiel's Wife

Read Ezekiel 24:15–27

H ave you ever lost a loved one? If you have, you will understand the pain involved. The prophet Ezekiel was married. All we know about his wife is recorded for us in this short passage of Scripture. We catch a glimpse here of the relationship that existed between Ezekiel and his wife.

God came to the prophet one day to tell him that he was going to take away the "desire" (KJV) or the "delight" (NIV) of his eyes (verse 16). This statement tells us a lot. Have you ever been surprised by the break-up of a marriage that you thought was going well? It is easy to let people think that things are going well in your marriage, while in fact they are going very badly. Human beings can put up a good front.

God, however, is never fooled. He reads the thoughts of our minds. He understands our hearts. He knows us better than we know ourselves. He sees what takes place when no one else is around. When God told Ezekiel that he was going to take away the delight of his eyes, he tells us a lot about what Ezekiel thought about his wife. Ezekiel's wife was a delight to him. Ezekiel treasured her and loved her very much. She brought much joy and happiness to his heart. He took pleasure in having her with him. The relationship between Ezekiel and his wife was a beautiful illustration of the relationship between God and his people. You see, God took great delight in his people too. He showered them with his blessings. He loved them very much. You can feel the pain that Ezekiel must have felt when he was told that God would take away his wife. This pain would not be unlike the pain that God felt in his heart when he punished his own people.

Notice how verse 16 tells us that "with one stroke" (NKJV) God would take away the desire of the heart of Ezekiel. Do you realize how quickly you could lose those things that are dear to your heart? In an instant they could be swept away from you. It is only by the grace of God that we have what we have. It is important for us to realize here that God has the right to take away those things he has given to us. How often we live as though God owed us something. The moment we gave our lives to Christ, we surrendered every personal right we believed we had. As believers, we do not have rights. We have died to self and yielded every right to God. Our rights were crucified with him on the cross. We no longer belong to ourselves. Everything we have is his to do with as he pleases. Are you willing to accept this? There can be no growth in the Christian life until we accept these conditions. Christ must have all of us. Ezekiel had to face this reality. God was going to take away his wife.

Mourning is a very normal response to the loss of a loved one. The Lord told the prophet Ezekiel, however, that he was not to mourn the loss of his wife. No tears were to be shed when his wife died. He was not to publicly display his grief. He was to act as if nothing had happened. Life was to go on as normal.

As God said, Ezekiel's wife died in the evening. He obeyed the voice of the Lord and went on with life as normal. People did not understand what was happening. They saw the prophet going about his daily routine as if nothing had happened. They saw him shed no tears. He did not show any grief over what had taken place. Obviously, they knew he loved his wife dearly, so they came to ask him why he reacted to the death of his wife in this manner.

Ezekiel now had the opportunity to explain to the people why the Lord took away his wife. God used the prophet's wife as an object lesson for his people. Soon God would take away the delight of their eyes. Their city, their temple, their children would all fall by the enemy's sword. They too would feel the pain of losing something that was very dear to them. Like Ezekiel, they would mourn privately among themselves (verse 23), but there would not be any public display of grief.

Why would they not publicly display their grief? Could it be because of fear? As their enemies led them into captivity, they were unable to display their grief. There in their land of exile they would not be given the right to grieve their loss in the customary way. They would be treated as slaves. There would be no time of mourning. They would be immediately put to work to serve the great Babylonian cause.

Verse 27 tells us that on the day that the Lord would bring to pass this word about his people, Ezekiel's mouth would be opened. He would no longer be silent. How are we to understand this? If we look at the rest of the book of Ezekiel, we find that the prophet no longer prophesied to the people of God about their coming judgment. In chapters 25–33 of his book, the prophet would speak to the nations. It would not be until chapter 33 that Ezekiel would again speak to God's people. This would be after the fall of Jerusalem. This would fulfill the prophecy that God had given Ezekiel through the death of his wife. When Ezekiel did speak again to God's people, it would no longer be with messages of doom and destruction. His messages would become messages of hope and restoration. With the death of his wife, Ezekiel ended his prophecies against the people of God.

How would you feel if you were the prophet Ezekiel? How would you react if you discovered that God had taken your loved one so she could serve as an object lesson for someone else? It would not be easy for the prophet to explain the meaning of the death of his wife to those who asked what it meant. What a powerful message it would have been, however. In spite of the pain it brought him, Ezekiel humbly submitted to the will of the Lord and preached one of the most difficult messages of his career as a priest and prophet. Would you have had his courage?

Sometimes the Lord leads us through deep valleys. Sometimes our path is steep and difficult. God's ways are not our ways. We cannot always understand God's purposes. As Lord, however, he has the right to do with us as he pleases for the purpose of drawing us closer to himself. Are you willing to accept whatever he sends your way? I remember the tragic death of a deacon in one of the churches I attended some time ago. This death sent shock waves throughout the entire church. The young people, in particular, were brought through this to a deeper awareness of the shortness of life. In the months that followed the death of this dear brother, young people began to come to church. There was a renewed interest in the things of the Lord. Knowing this brother as I did, if he had known that his death would mean spiritual renewal for these young people, he would have willingly died for their renewal. Somehow I believe that Ezekiel's wife would have felt the same. I can only pray that I would have the same willingness.

For Consideration:

- What rights do we really have as believers? Do we really live as though we have given all our rights to the Lord?

- Would you be able to surrender to the Lord those things in which your heart delights? What would you find most difficult to surrender?

- Has God ever taken something from you that you delighted in? How did he use this for your good and his glory?

For Prayer:

- Confess to the Lord your inability to surrender all to him.

- Ask the Lord to help you to surrender all.

- Offer your life to him afresh for him to use as he sees fit.

- Thank him that you can trust what he is doing, even though you do not always understand.

26

Love Your Enemies

Read Ezekiel 25

What do you do when your enemy falls? We all know what our natural response might be. The Bible tells us what our response should be: "Love your enemies and pray for those who persecute you" (Matthew 5:44). This does not come naturally to us. In the passage before us, we see the response of the nations toward the fall of God's people. There are four nations addressed in this chapter. Each of the nations responds in a different way. Let us consider the examples before us.

Ammon (1–7)
   The first nation mentioned here is the nation of Ammon. What was the response of the people of Ammon to the fall of Jerusalem? Our passage tells us that they cried, "Aha!" This was an expression of joy. When they saw the desecration of the temple, they rejoiced. When they saw the land being turned into a wasteland, they were happy. They were glad

when they saw the people of God being led off into captivity. Verse 6 tells us that the Ammonites clapped their hands and stamped their feet in joy when God's people were led away.

We have to admit that the people of God deserved what they got. They had turned their backs on God. Though God had warned them many times, they refused to listen. This did not give Ammon the right to rejoice in their destruction, however. God was not pleased with their attitude toward the fall of Jerusalem. He would hand them over to an enemy from the east. This enemy would eat their bread and take over their land. Their great cities would be abandoned and turned into pasture land for camels and sheep. They would be destroyed as a people because they had rejoiced in the downfall of God's people.

When your enemy falls, do you rejoice? They may have been in the wrong. They may have even made your life miserable. Rejoicing at their downfall, however, is not what God wants from us. How we need God's grace to feel the needs and pains of our enemies! Though we were once ourselves the enemies of God, he had compassion on us. He sent his son to die for us while we were wallowing in our rebellion. His love transcended our animosity and hatred. He looked beyond the sin and evil and saw the person beneath. He loved us even while we were his enemies. Shall we, who have experienced the compassion of God, rejoice at the downfall of our enemies? God reserved a serious punishment for the Ammonites. This shows us how seriously God takes this matter.

Moab (8–11)

Notice second the response of the nation of Moab: "Judah has become like all the other nations" (verse 8). What was she saying? Was she not saying something like this? "Look at them. They claim to be the people of God, and now look at what has happened to them. They are no better than we are.

Their God is no better than our gods. They thought they were something special, but they are not."

Moab adopted a critical attitude toward her enemy. Not only did she rejoice in the downfall of God's people, but also she began to criticize them. She openly mocked them in their time of trouble. She had an "I-told-you-so" mentality. How easy it is to develop such an attitude. This attitude not only rejoices in the downfall of the enemy, but it also rubs salt into their wounds. Those who have such an attitude kick their enemies when they are down. Have you ever found yourself in this situation? Do not allow yourself the right to judge and condemn your enemy. God alone is judge. Because of her attitude, Moab too would be handed over to her enemies (verse 10). May God not have to do this to us to help us see the error of our ways.

Edom (12–14)

The third response came from the Edomites. God was going to lay waste to their cities. He would take vengeance on them. Why was God so angry with Edom? Edom had taken revenge on the people of God (verse 12). Listen to what the Edomites cried out when Jerusalem fell: "Tear it down, tear it down to its foundations" (Psalm 137:7). Ezekiel 35:5 tells us that the Edomites "shed the blood of the children of Israel by the force of the sword in the time of their calamity, in the time that their iniquity had an end" (KJV). Obadiah the prophet describes for us in greater detail what Edom did when Jerusalem fell:

On the day you stood aloof
    while strangers carried off his wealth
    and foreigners entered his gates
    and cast lots for Jerusalem,
    you were like one of them.

You should not look down on your brother
    in the day of his misfortune,
nor rejoice over the people of Judah
    in the day of their destruction,
nor boast so much
    in the day of their trouble.

You should not march through the gates of my people
    in the day of their disaster,
nor look down on them in their calamity
    in the day of their disaster,
nor seize their wealth
    in the day of their disaster.

You should not wait at the crossroads
    to cut down their fugitives,
nor hand over their survivors
    in the day of their trouble.
(Obadiah, verses 11–14)

Edom not only rejoiced and criticized the people of God in the day of their destruction, but she also helped the enemy destroy them. She joined forces with the enemy. The Edomites would not have attempted such a thing by themselves, but when they saw they could get away with it, they took advantage of the situation by helping Babylon destroy Judah.

How easy it is to get caught up in such a sin! What do you do when people all around you are gossiping and criticizing another person? Is it not easy to join in and do the same thing yourself? While we would not particularly want to be the source of such gossip, we do feel quite comfortable in joining others in the attack. If worse came to worse, we could always say that it was someone else who started it. You cannot excuse your actions by hiding behind someone else. God will hold you accountable for your own sin.

Philistia (15–17)

The final example we have here is the example of Philistia. This was a nation that openly sought to destroy the people of God. The Philistines did not hide behind the Babylonians, as did the Edomites. The Philistines were outspoken enemies of God's people. While it is sometimes easier to recognize and deal with obvious enemies, they are still very dangerous. Many of us do not have the courage to show our inner face when it comes to our feelings about another person. We would prefer to hide our true feelings. At least with these blatant enemies, we know where we stand. They are not hypocrites. This does not make them any better, however. They will be punished for their sins as well. Notice what God said would happen to them: "And I will execute great vengeance upon them with furious rebukes; and they shall know that I am the LORD, when I shall lay my vengeance upon them" (verse 17 KJV).

We have seen in this chapter four different responses toward the downfall of the people of God. What do we need to learn from this chapter? Do we not need to examine ourselves in light of these nations? What is our response toward our enemies and their misfortunes? Does the love of Christ shine brightly in our lives for our enemies? How often have we been found guilty of the same crimes as these nations? May God grant us the ability to love our enemies, even as Christ loved us.

For Consideration:

- Do you have people in your life that rub you the wrong way? What is your response to them when they are in pain or suffering?

- What should our response be when our enemy suffers?

- Take a moment to consider how you may be guilty of the same crimes as the nations here in this chapter.

For Prayer:

- Take a moment to thank the Lord for his love toward you, even when you were his enemy.

- Do you know someone who is difficult for you to love? Who in particular? Ask God for grace to love that person as he loves you.

27

Materialistic Tyre

Read Ezekiel 26

In chapters 26–28 Ezekiel prophesied against the region of Tyre. Historians tell us that Tyre was a very important commercial center at the time of Ezekiel. It boasted of two excellent harbors where ships could come with their supplies for trade. The city itself was built around one of these harbors. The second harbor was located on an offshore island connected to the mainland by a causeway. Foreign ships brought their goods regularly for trade to this great city. Materialism abounded as merchants and traders gathered to make their fortunes.

Evidence of Tyre's love for material possessions can be found in her response to the downfall of the city of Jerusalem: "I shall be filled; she is laid waste" (verse 2 NKJV). Jerusalem had been a prosperous city. Now that she had fallen, her trade would go to Tyre. Tyre rejoiced because Jerusalem's fate would lead to her prosperity.

Tyre feels no compassion for Israel in her need. Her

only concern was to profit from Israel's misery. Materialism elevates the importance of *things* and depreciates the value of people. We cringe when we read about the child sacrifices that took place in the Old Testament worship of Baal. We fail to realize, however, that we can be guilty of the same sin. How often have our children been placed on the altar and offered as sacrifices to the god of materialism? How often have we placed our spouses on that same altar? To honor the god of materialism, we willingly sacrifice our relationships with our families and friends. Possessions and money become our central focus. The god of materialism delights in human sacrifice. You don't have to look very far to find those who worship at the Church of Materialism.

The Bible tells us that when Nebuchadnezzar invaded Jerusalem he destroyed the city. 2 Kings 25 records the cruelty of this invasion. Nebuchadnezzar burned down important buildings. He plucked out the eyes of the king after slaughtering his sons in front of him. Famine resulting from the siege of the city forced parents to eat the bodies of their own children to survive. Pregnant women had their bellies ripped open by the sword. People were driven from their homes by the point of the sword. There was tremendous loss of life. Tyre cared nothing about this. The only concern she had was how to tap into the money that was now available because Israel was out of the way. The god of materialism had deadened Tyre's senses. We can expect nothing less from our materialism.

Notice the response of God to the materialism of Tyre. In verse 3 God used language that the people of Tyre could understand. They were a people who lived by the sea. They saw boats in their harbor on a daily basis. It was for this reason that the Lord told them that he would come upon them like a great wave sweeping over a boat. That wave of judgment would sweep over them. It would crash down on their walls and break down their strong towers (verse 4).

That wave would leave them as barren and desolate as the top of a great rock (verse 4). Their wealth, their stores, and their beautiful homes would all disappear. They would become the plunder of the nations (verse 5). The neighboring villages around Tyre would also know the devastating consequences of their own sin. They too would be slain by the sword as their enemies crashed down on them like a wave in all its fury.

In verse 7 the Lord told Tyre that he would bring the nation of Babylon against them. This was the nation that had devastated Judah. Tyre would suffer the same judgment. The horses and chariots of Babylon would slay them. They would break down their walls and strong towers. The dust from the vast numbers of Babylonian chariots and horses would fill their land. The citizens of Tyre would be trampled by the hooves of these great war horses. The possessions they loved so much would be plundered and taken from them. Their "pleasant houses" would lie in ruins (verse 12). The music and songs that formed so much of the materialistic culture of Tyre would no longer be heard (verse 13). Instead, there would be the uncomfortable silence of death. She would be destroyed as a nation, never to be rebuilt again.

This is the ultimate destiny of a materialistic society. The god of materialism is never satisfied. After taking all he can get through you, he will then take all he can get from you and leave you empty and barren. Stories abound of those who, after reaching the height of success, found that they were left destitute and barren in the end.

Notice the response of the surrounding nations to what had happened to Tyre (verses 15–16). They were astonished that the mighty Tyre had fallen. Never had it entered their minds that such a city would fall. They trembled for fear because of what had happened to Tyre. I am convinced that Tyre herself could not believe what had happened to her. She had been so prosperous and secure. Never had it entered her mind that she could lose all she had worked so hard to obtain. We should never take the blessings we have for granted. At best, those blessings are hanging from a spider's thread. One breath of the Almighty, and they come crashing to the ground.

Verses 17 and 18 are a lament. This righteous prophecy of doom was written as a reminder to the generations to come of the dangers of materialism and the insecurity of trusting in the things of this world. She who was once the envy and terror of the nations was no more.

In verses 19–21 we read that the destiny of Tyre was to perish eternally. She would be brought down to the "pit." That pit was a place of eternal death. There would be no return for her. All her hopes and dreams of the future would be abruptly shattered. Paul tells Timothy in 1 Timothy 6:10: "For the love of money is a root of all kinds of evil. Some people, eager for money, have wandered from the faith and pierced themselves with many griefs."

Materialism was the downfall of the city of Tyre. Her love for money and possessions drove her to the grave. She was confident in herself, her abilities, and wealth. She had reached the top of the heap. She was the envy of the world, but now she was absolutely empty. Maybe you have been trapped in the worship of this same god. Heed the warning of this passage. This passage is a warning to all who would follow the footsteps of Tyre. Surrender yourself to the Lord today. Confess your sin. In God alone is there security.

For Consideration:

- We have mentioned here that the god of materialism is a god who requires human sacrifice. Do you agree with this statement? Give some examples of this from your experience. How have people in your life been sacrificed in an attempt to gain more wealth and prosperity?

- How much security can this world really bring us? How easy would it be for us to lose everything we have worked so hard to obtain?

- Why is materialism so attractive?

- Where does materialism leave us in the end?

For Prayer:

- Have you been guilty of sacrificing someone in your pursuit of materialism? Ask the Lord to forgive you and show you what you need to do to make things right.

- Thank the Lord that in him alone there is security.

- Consider what the Lord has given you over your lifetime. Take a moment to recognize that without him none of this would be possible. Thank and worship him for what he has given you. Be specific in your prayers.

28

Tyre the Great

Read Ezekiel 27

From the last chapter we saw that Tyre was a very rich and prosperous nation. Chapters 27 and 28 go to great lengths to describe for us the affluence of Tyre. She had everything she could have possibly hoped for. She was deprived of nothing her world had to offer. She was the envy of the nations of the world. She could boast of wealth, riches, ease, and prosperity. Where did all of this lead her in the end? Chapter 27 paints for us a picture of a nation whose greatness destroyed her. Ultimately, this chapter causes us to examine our own priorities in life.

Let's consider what this chapter tells us about the greatness of Tyre. We discover from verse 3 that Tyre was situated on the seacoast. Her location was one of the key reasons for her success as a thriving commercial center. Verse 3 makes mention of the merchants who came to do business at the great seaports of Tyre. The city itself was a very beautiful place (verses 3–4). The inhabitants of Tyre knew that their city was lovely, and they boasted of her perfected beauty. Her man-made structures and buildings seemed to enhance her natural splendor. God compared her to a great sailing ship. This was a language she could understand. Ships were the source of her livelihood. The inhabitants of Tyre had seen their share of ships. They could identify with this imagery. As a great ship, Tyre was built from the best material available in her day. Her body was made from the fir trees of Senir (verse 5). Her mast was carved out of a great cedar of Lebanon (verse 5). She was propelled at sea by oars made from the strong oak trees of Bashan (verse 6). Her deck was laid out with ivory from the coasts of Cyprus (verse 6). She proudly displayed her sails made from fine embroidered linen imported from Egypt (verse 7). She was covered with the blue and purple fabric of Elishah (verse 7). Skilled oarsmen from Sidon and Arvad sailed her through the seas (verse 8). She was piloted by her great wise men (verse 9). The wise men and elders of Gebal caulked her seams (verse 9). Soldiers and skilled warriors from Persia, Lydia, and Put guarded her and bravely adorned her with shields and helmets commemorating her many conquests (verse 10). Men of Arvad and Helech guarded her walls (verse 11). What a great city she was! She had the best of everything. She lacked nothing.

Tyre traded with all the nations around her. Verses 12–24 give us a list of her trading partners. From Tarshish she obtained her wealth of silver, iron, tin, and lead (verse 12). She bartered with Greece, Tubal, and Meshech for slaves and bronze (verse 13). From the house of Togarmah, she obtained work horses, war horses, and mules (verse 14). For services rendered, Rhodes supplied her with ivory tusks and ebony (verse 15). In return for her wares, Aram (Syria) gave her emeralds, purple fabric, embroidered work, fine linen, coral, and rubies (verse 16). Judah and Israel traded wheat, millet, honey, oil, and balm with her (verse 17). Damascus provided her with wine and wool (verse 18). Dan and Greece paid for their supplies with iron, cassia, and cane (calamus). Dedan was her source of saddlecloth for riding (verse 20). Arabia and Kedar traded her for lambs, rams, and goats (verse 21). Sheba and Raamah furnished her with precious stones, spices, and gold (verse 22). Haran, Canneh, Eden, Sheba, Asshur, and Kilmad outfitted her with garments, blue fabric, embroidered work, and multicolored rugs with knotted cords. Tyre was the place to go if you were looking for something to buy. Here you could have a choice of the finest wares available anywhere in the world. She was one of the most important commercial centers in the world of her day.

Materially speaking, she was a very prosperous nation. Her goods were being carried to the far corners of the globe by ships from Tarshish (verse 25). She was a wealthy and glorious nation (verse 25). With all this wealth and prosperity, you would have thought that her future would have been secure. What could bring her down now? There seemed to be no end to her prosperity and influence. Her downfall would cause world-wide economic chaos.

This prosperity would not last forever. In verse 26 Ezekiel painted a picture of this great ship, Tyre, in the middle of the ocean loaded with her goods. The east wind came up and beat against her side. The force of that east wind was so great that she was broken in two. Her riches, merchandise, sailors, soldiers, and entire crew fell into the sea (verse 27). Here was a nation that thought she had everything going for her. There was nothing that could bring her down. Her future was secure—at least that is what she thought.

What a warning this is to us today! At best, our possessions are hanging from a spider's web. In an instant the east wind could blow and remove everything we have from us. What guarantee do you have of tomorrow? What guarantee do you really have that when you wake up in the morning, you will not lose everything you worked so hard to achieve? In an age of nuclear weapons and chemical warfare, is it not somewhat foolish to assume that what we have is absolutely secure?

The fall of Tyre would send shock waves throughout the entire world. The land would shake at the cry of her drowning pilots (verse 28). The great sailors of the sea would cast anchor off the coast of Tyre and stand in awe at the sight of a once glorious city now devastated (verse 29). The world would be in mourning because of the fall of this once great nation. The nations would cry bitterly, put dust on their heads, shave themselves bald, and wear sackcloth, weeping and wailing for the devastation of Tyre (verses 30–32). Never had it entered their minds that such a thing would happen to such a great nation. Tyre had satisfied many people and enriched kings with her luxuries, but now she lay broken at the bottom of the sea. Her wealth and possessions lay there with her. Tyre's riches could not protect her from the anger of the God of Israel. She had everything this world could offer but perished because she was not right with God. Now Tyre would be remembered not because of her great wealth and prosperity but because of her fall. The once glorious nation would be no more.

How quickly we take our prosperity for granted. We fail to realize, were it not for Almighty God, we would have nothing. We become secure in our possessions and find ourselves drifting away from God. While we would never admit it, our lifestyles reflect the belief that we can make it on our own. We can all too easily be sucked up into the vacuum of materialism and self-sufficiency. May God cause us to learn the lesson Tyre had to learn before it is too late.

For Consideration:

- Take a moment to consider if you have been caught up in the glory of materialism. Do you feel its pull? Give some examples.

- What warning do you take from this chapter? Is there anything that needs to change in your life?

For Prayer:

- Thank God for his provision for your needs.

- Ask him to reveal to you any way in which you have fallen into the trap of Tyre.

- Ask him to change your priorities in life.

29

Woe to
the King of Tyre

Read Ezekiel 28

In this chapter God concluded his prophetic words to
Tyre. He addressed the king of Tyre in this section. Let's
consider what God had to say about this great man.

Notice how the king of Tyre saw himself. Verse 2
tells us that he was a very proud man. He saw himself as
a god. He was the leader of one of the most prosperous
nations on the earth at that time. He basked in the wealth
that constantly flowed into the port each day. He felt that
nothing could harm him. He had everything he needed. His
riches had gone to his head. God reminded him through the
prophet Ezekiel that he was still merely a man.

Not only did the king see himself as a god, he also
considered himself to be a very wise man. He lifted himself
up above his people. He claimed to be wiser than Daniel
(one of the Israelite wise men who lived in exile in Babylon
during the reign of King Nebuchadnezzar). Daniel had been
so wise that the king of Babylon had made him the chief of

all the Babylonian wise men. The king of Tyre claimed here to have a wisdom superior to that of Daniel. He claimed that the evidence of his wisdom was the wealth that had accumulated in his city. He believed that it was because of his wise administration that Tyre was so wealthy.

It was to this proud man that the Word of the Lord came. Because he had lifted himself up to be a god before his people, strangers would be sent to invade his land (verse 7). These foreigners would come from the most terrible nations. They would come with one purpose in mind—to destroy the city with all its beauty and splendor (verse 7). Tyre would perish with all her wealth. According to verse 8 she would go down to the pit and die a horrible death in the middle of the sea. Historians tell us that the old city of Tyre is now beneath the sea, even as God promised.

What would be the king's response to the judgment of God? Would he say to those who were slaying him that he was a god (verse 9)? He would be shown for what he really was—a mere man. Death has a way of humbling even the greatest men and women. Here our strength, wisdom, and pride are all stripped from us. We are reduced to a lifeless bag of flesh and bones. As powerful and as wise as he was, the king of Tyre could not stand before the judgment of God. We will all stand one day before God (Romans 14:10). On that day it will not matter how much money, power, or wealth we have. All that will matter is our relationship with God. The king of Tyre serves as a powerful lesson to us of the importance of being ready to face our God.

Ezekiel was called on to prophesy that God's righteous judgment would come against the king of Tyre.[1] Ezekiel spoke here from the point of view of the king of Tyre, that is, from the perspective of how he saw himself. Ezekiel described him as the "model of perfection" (at least that is how the king liked to see himself), though we know from the context that he was far from this (verse 11). He was full of wisdom, beauty, and perfection (at least that was the impression he liked to give others). He lived in the Garden of Eden surrounded by every precious stone imaginable (verse 13). When Ezekiel referred here to the Garden of Eden, he spoke in poetic language. He compared Tyre to the Garden of Eden because of its beauty and perfection. As king he was the anointed "cherub who covers" (NKJV) or "guardian cherub" (NIV). He lived, as it were, on the very mountain of God, in the glory of the presence of God. He was perfect in all his ways until he fell. We should not take this literally. Ezekiel was speaking in poetic language here. The king of Tyre was a mere man who considered himself to be a god. He considered himself to be perfect in all his ways. He was in reality, however, a man who fell deeply into sin and iniquity. He became filled with violence because of the abundance of his trading (verse 16). The god of materialism had overcome him. He was obsessed with himself and his possessions. Because of this the guardian cherub was cast away from the presence of God. He was taken from among the fiery stones (verse 16). Could this be a reference to the precious stones and wealth he had amassed? All this would amount to nothing in the end.

His heart was lifted up in pride because of his beauty (verse 17). He corrupted the wisdom God had given him by using it for himself and his own evil ways. Because of this he was cast to the ground for others to gaze upon. There on the ground all his splendor and glory would be stripped from him. Notice in verse 18 that the king of Tyre had no use for faith. He defiled the sanctuaries by his many sins. He had no time for God. He was too busy amassing wealth. God would send a fire against him. That fire would reduce him to ashes in the sight of those who watched (verse 18). Everyone who knew him would be astonished at his downfall (verse 19). One of the greatest men on the surface of the earth would be reduced to nothing by the hand of Almighty God. Everyone would see that God laughs at the great strength and wisdom of people. Before God the greatest of people are but fleas.

In verses 20–26 God spoke to the neighboring city of Sidon. God would also be glorified in this city. He would send pestilence against her. Blood would run in her streets. A sword would come against her from all sides. She too would be judged. She would be judged because she had been "painful briers and sharp thorns" to the house of Israel. God was not blind to the things she had done to his people. He would judge Sidon for her sins against his children.

Ezekiel concluded this section with a prophetic word about the people of God who had been in exile (verses 25–26). He prophesied that they would again be gathered together and return to their own land. There they would dwell in safety and know the blessing of God as he prospered their land. He tells us that God would execute judgment upon all those nations who despised his people. While this is a particular promise to the nation of Israel as his people, it is also a promise to us as believers today. God does not turn a blind eye to what is happening to his children. We are precious to him and he loves us dearly.

What does this section have to do with us today? Here before us we see the picture of a great king. The god of materialism destroyed him. Love for possessions and the easy life drove him away from God. How quickly we take God for granted in our prosperity. We fail to realize that, were it not for Almighty God, we would not be able to work to provide for our families. How we need to realize that, as God did in Tyre, so he could do with us. How quickly he could remove his blessings from us. Let us not take him for granted. Let us praise him and thank him for his blessings toward us on a daily basis. Do not let your material possessions rob you of an understanding of how dependent you are on your God.

For Consideration:

- Why do you suppose the king of Tyre had such a high view of himself? Was any of this justified?

- Is it possible for us to fall into the same trap today? Give some examples of how we can puff ourselves up.

- Is it possible that even in our churches we can become proud of the size of our congregations and the gifts of our people?

For Prayer:

- Ask God to help you see that there is really nothing in yourself that you can boast about because everything you have comes from his hand.

- Ask him to forgive you for the times you believed that it was because of your wisdom and your strength that you achieved some goal.

- Take a moment to thank the Lord for his wisdom and his strength. Recognize him as the source of all these blessings.

30

The Fall of a Great Nation

Read Ezekiel 29

The nation of Egypt was another powerful and influential nation in her time. Even in our day we marvel at her culture and achievements. The wonder of the pyramids still entices many people in our modern age. We stand in awe of the great wealth of her past. Her pharaohs have gone down in history as some of the world's most influential men. Chapters 29–32 of Ezekiel were dedicated to this great nation of Egypt. God had much to say to her.

In Ezekiel 29 the prophet used two illustrations to describe Egypt. The first of these illustrations was that of a great sea monster (verses 3–6). There are a few things we need to notice here about this monster. Notice first that this monster claimed that the river Nile was his. The Nile was a picture of the nation of Egypt. In the last meditation we saw how God compared Tyre to a great ship (because she was a port city). The illustration of the river was very appropriate for Egypt because the Nile River ran through her land and was the source of her wealth.

We see here that this great monster claimed that he had made the river and it was his. Pharaoh was a very proud individual. He believed that the greatness of Egypt was because of his own wisdom and skilled administration. How easy it is for us to believe that we are indispensable. It is easy to feel that we are where we are today because of our own skills and talents. What Pharaoh failed to realize was that were it not for the God of Israel, he would have nothing. Even unbelievers are absolutely dependent upon God for all they have and all they have achieved.

Notice in verse 4 that the smaller fish of the Nile clung to the scales of this Egyptian sea monster. While we are not told who these smaller fish were, it is evident that they were devoted to Egypt. They admired her strength and power. They clung to her for protection.

God was against Egypt. In verse 4 he tells her that he would put great hooks in her jaws and fish her out of the Nile like a skilled fisherman. He would then take her to a desert location and leave her to perish in the sun. There she would perish along with all her followers who clung to her scales. The wild birds of the air would come by and pick at the decaying remains of a once great nation. Her pride would be crushed. When this happened, everyone would know that the God of Israel was the one true God. Pharaoh, though he claimed to be god, was a mere man.

In the second illustration, Ezekiel compared Egypt to a reed (verse 6–7). We read in Jeremiah 41–42 how the people of God fled to Egypt for help in their time of trouble. Egypt, however, proved to be a broken reed for the people of God. When God's people leaned on the reed for support, it broke, tearing open their shoulder and wrenching their back. The reed of Egypt was no support for God's people in their hour of need. There are many reeds we can lean on today. Our money, our church, and our family are all examples of these reeds. What we need to learn here is that what may appear to be secure, in reality, will leave us barren and dry in the end. God alone can be our security. Israel had to learn this the hard way.

This great nation, which had been the pride of the earth, was now going to feel the sword of God's judgment. The flourishing delta of the Nile would become a desert (verse 9). Verse 9 tells us that God would reduce Egypt to a wasteland because she had boasted in her own greatness. Pride is a terrible sin in the eyes of God. For forty years Egypt would be desolate (verses 11–12). For forty years neither man nor beast would pass through this once prosperous nation. She would suffer what God's people suffered. She too would be invaded and taken captive. She too would be scattered over the face of the earth by the Babylonians. For forty years her land would be the home of wild animals. After these forty years, however, she would be returned to her land (verses 13–14). She would never again be great, however. She would remain a lowly kingdom (verse 14). Never again would she inspire the confidence of the world, as she had done in the days of Ezekiel (verse 16). To this day, this prophecy remains true. Egypt has never regained the power and influence she once had as a nation. The Bible tells us the reason for this judgment was her pride. The nation of Egypt is a constant example to us today of the danger of pride and self-confidence.

In verses 17–20 God shows us just how this prophecy would be fulfilled. Nebuchadnezzar, king of Babylon, would come against Egypt. God had used him as an instrument of judgment against Israel and Judah. In chapters 26–28 we saw that he had also been God's instrument to punish Tyre. Now he would invade Egypt and conquer her too. Notice here in verse 18 that the siege of Tyre was not easy for Nebuchadnezzar. Commentators tell us that this siege lasted for thirteen years. When Babylon did finally conquer Tyre, she had spent so much on the battle that she really got nothing from the conquest. Notice the imagery of hard work here in verse 18. As an army they had laboured strenuously against Tyre. They had gone bald in the process of conquering the land, and their shoulders were raw from the heavy load they had carried during those years of conquest. This would not be the case with Egypt. Egypt would be given to Nebuchadnezzar as a gift. The battle for Egypt was a battle that would increase the wealth of Babylon. Here Nebuchadnezzar would receive his wages from God for being his servant in exercising judgment on the nations.

When this prophecy took place, God would once again cause a "horn" to grow in Israel (verse 21). God would restore the power of his own people. The fall of Egypt was a sign of the times. When Israel saw the nation of Egypt fall, she would know that her deliverance was near. At that time God told Ezekiel that his mouth would be opened, and he would once again speak to Israel as he had done before (verse 21). This corresponded perfectly with what God had already told the prophet in Ezekiel 24:25–27. We understand from this that for a period of time, the prophet Ezekiel would not speak to God's people. Only after the fall of Egypt would God again send Ezekiel to the house of Israel to speak his Word. As a prophet Ezekiel had to learn when to be silent and when to speak the Word of God. He was only to speak as God led him to speak. There is, I believe, a lesson here for us. Do we have enough discernment to recognize the leading of the Lord in our lives? How many times have we spoken when we should have been silent or been silent when we should have spoken? May God give us the discernment to know the difference.

For Consideration:

- What do we learn from this chapter about pride and the danger of pride?

- Have you ever felt the temptation to be proud? In what areas of your life are you most tempted to be proud?

- Is it possible that what happened to Egypt could also happen to us or our nation? What are the things we place our confidence in today?

For Prayer:

- Take a moment to consider where you would be today without the Lord. Give him praise for what he has done in your life.

- Pray that God would protect you from this great sin of pride. Confess any pride in your life right now and ask God to give you his humility.

- Have you ever been tempted to speak when you should not have spoken? Have you ever remained silent when you should have spoken? Ask God to help you to know the difference.

31

A Sword for Egypt

Read Ezekiel 30

Egypt's strength had captivated the attention of many people. Even the Israelites had benefited from her blessing in the time of Joseph. We saw in the last meditation that the Pharaoh had become very proud of what he had. He honestly believed that it was because of his own skill and administration that the nation had become what it was in his day. He had a very powerful influence in the world of his time. Egypt felt secure because of her prosperity.

In this chapter God again told Ezekiel to prophesy judgment on the people of Egypt. Notice in verse 2 that he was to "wail" because of what was about to happen to her. Her day of judgment was very near. That day would be a very dark day in the history of Egypt. It is described in the NKJV as being the *time of the Gentiles*, a day of judgment for the unbelieving Gentile world. Egypt had lived her life in prosperity and fame. Now her judgment had come. She was not ready for this day. It was a day of terrible judgment. Her money and prosperity would mean nothing to her on this day.

A great sword was about to fall on this mighty nation. It was the sword of God's judgment. There would be anguish in Cush (Ethiopia, NKJV). When that sword fell upon Egypt, it would strip her of her wealth. Her inhabitants would be slain and her foundations brought to the ground (verse 4). All those things her people had delighted in (her architecture and her wealth) would amount to nothing in the end. Egyptians would be stripped bare and left naked before the God of this universe to answer to him for how they had lived their lives.

Notice in verses 5 and 6 that not only would Egypt fall but so would all those who had allied themselves with her. These people had marvelled at the glory of Egypt. They had flocked to her because of her wealth and influence. Egypt had seduced them and led them astray. Now they too would suffer along with Egypt. Let it never be said that your sins affect only yourself. The fact of the matter is that we all touch the lives of others in some way or another. What kind of influence have you had on those you rub shoulders with on a regular basis? Will they perish too because of what they have seen in your life?

Verses 7–9 describe for us that horrible end for those who had fallen because of Egypt's bad example. These lands would be desolate and ruined (verse 7). They would be burned to the ground and crushed (verse 8). Verse 9 tells us that anguish would take hold of them. What a terrible end lay in store for those who had fallen prey to Egypt's seduction. Egypt was leading her admirers straight to hell. How many people have turned their backs on the only hope they have of eternal life because of the bad example they have seen in believers today? What guilt Egypt had to bear! How these verses challenge us to live for the Lord and be good witnesses for him, so we don't carry the guilt of Egypt on our shoulders.

Notice in verse 9 how God told Ezekiel that he would send a messenger to Ethiopia (Cush) to frighten them out of their complacency or carelessness (NKJV). Does that messenger need to come to us today? How many times have we as believers become complacent and careless in our witness for the Lord Jesus? How many times have we felt secure in our traditions and religious activities yet found ourselves spiritually asleep? How we need to be awakened to the reality of the battle before us and the ultimate destiny of those who have turned their backs on the Lord. How we need to be revived and renewed in our walk with God. Notice here that God does not judge Ethiopia without warning her. He sent his messenger to bring her to himself, but she refused to listen.

God would execute this great judgment on Egypt by means of the nation of Babylon (see verses 10–12). The Babylonian army was the most feared of all armies. They were known for their might and cruelty (verse 11). They would sweep down on Egypt and her friends and destroy them. The glory of Egypt would effectively come to an end. The land would be filled with the slain of Egypt (verse 12). The judgment of God would dry up the Nile River (verse 12). It would be evident to all that the hand of God was against them.

Verses 13–19 described in greater detail the devastation that would occur on the day of God's judgment. The idols of Memphis would be brought to an end (verse 13). The reign of Egypt's proud princes would be terminated (verse 13). The whole nation would be cast under the shadow of fear (verse 13). Once they had felt secure in their belief that their great Pharaoh could protect them. Now they were in terror of their enemies. Upper Egypt would be left desolate and Zoan would be burned to the ground (verse 14). The city of Thebes would be punished; it would be "taken by storm" and many of its inhabitants would be killed (verses 14–16). The great city of Pelusium would experience the full force of the wrath of God and writhe in anguish (verses 15–16). Memphis would be in daily distress (verse 16). The young men of Heliopolis and Bubastis would fall by the sword of God's judgment, and the inhabitants of their cities would go into captivity. They would not be able to defend their cities against the great army of Babylon (verse 17). It would be a very dark day for Egypt when the Lord brought his judgment on her. Ezekiel prophesied that the Egyptians would be taken from their land and forced into captivity (just like Israel and Judah). All this would be done in such a way that the land of Egypt would have to realize that the God of Israel was the one true God (verse 19).

God gave Ezekiel a picture in verses 20–26. He spoke here of breaking Pharaoh's arms. The "breaking of Pharaoh's arm" referred to his being weakened. With one arm broken, Pharaoh was not the powerful man he once was. This may have referred to an initial attack of Babylon that left the Egyptians in such a weakened state that they could not repair the damages or bandage their wounds. While Egypt was suffering from one broken arm, God would again attack. This time the other arm would be broken as well, and Egypt would be left absolutely powerless. Her sword would fall out of her hands (she would have no defense against the God of Israel). As a nation she would be scattered throughout the other nations. In order to accomplish his purposes, God would strengthen the hands of the king of Babylon. Through this evil king, God would judge Egypt for her sin.

As influential and powerful as she was, Egypt fell. She fell because she had become a very proud people. She fell so that God could show her that he was God. Her kings claimed to be gods. They were proven to be mere men. The sad part of this story is that many people had fallen into Egypt's trap. They believed in Pharaoh, his power and influence. They trusted him, but they were destroyed in the end. How many times have we become followers of people and not of God? We cannot afford to place our trust in people. God alone is worthy of our absolute confidence. How many individuals had Egypt's life touched? How many people had she intoxicated with her lust for power and wealth? I wonder how many people have been affected by my negative attitudes and actions. May God grant us the grace to influence those around us for good and not evil.

For Consideration:

- What does this chapter teach us about the importance of our witness for Christ in the eyes of the world?

- What kind of a witness have you been to those around you?

- Have you ever found yourself being drawn to particular individuals and their teaching? Why is it dangerous to place your trust in people?

For Prayer:

- Ask God to give you a greater understanding of the ultimate destiny of those who do not know the Lord.

- Ask God to help you to be a true and faithful witness to those you come in contact with on an ongoing basis.

- Thank God that he alone is worthy of our complete confidence.

- Do you know individuals who have become followers of people and not of God? Pray that God would open their eyes.

32

The Example of Assyria

Read Ezekiel 31

Tragedy is something that is supposed to happen to someone else. It is never supposed to happen to us. At least that is what we think until someone close to us suffers a tragedy. Then we are forced into the reality that it could happen to us as well. Egypt was big and powerful enough that she believed that nothing could really happen to her. God was aware of this false hope she was clinging to and gave her an example of another great nation that felt the same way. God gave Egypt this example so she would realize that judgment could indeed fall on her as well.

Notice in verse 2 that the Lord asked Pharaoh the question: "Whom are you like in your greatness?" This question shows us what Egypt was thinking about herself. She was a great nation. She felt, however, that her greatness could protect her. God was about to give her a lesson in history that would prove that greatness did not guarantee freedom from judgment.

God used the example of the nation of Assyria. He compared Assyria in verse 3 to a tall cedar of Lebanon. Notice what he said about this tall cedar tree. It had fine branches that shaded the forest. Many people enjoyed the shade of its protection. It was a very tall tree and stood out among the trees of the forest. Assyria, at one point in her history, was the most powerful nation on the earth.

This great cedar of Assyria was well-watered. As a nation she enjoyed the abundance of God's blessing. Many people profited from Assyria's prosperity. She sent out channels to the surrounding trees of the forest (verse 4). The nation of Assyria was "exalted above all the trees of the field" (verse 5 NKJV). There was not a nation that could be compared to her in her day. Her branches became long as she extended her borders. Her boughs multiplied as she conquered more and more nations and forced them into submission (verse 5). Many nations made their homes under the shelter of the branches of this great cedar tree. They were submissive to Assyria and paid her homage. Even the birds of the air made their nests in her branches. Everyone owed much to this great and prosperous nation of Assyria. The other cedar trees, the pine trees, or the plane trees could not match her beauty and strength (verse 8). Such was the blessing of God on Assyria. She was the envy of all the trees of the garden (verse 9).

Notice, however, what happened to this great and magnificent cedar tree. Verse 10 tells us that she became very proud. It is never easy to be on the top. Satan seems to target those who are prosperous and successful. How many people have climbed to the top only to fall down the other side because of pride? When things are going good, beware of the attack of the enemy. This is what happened to Assyria. In her wealth and prosperity, she turned her back on God. This is also the story of God's people. When everything seemed to be going well for them, they were quick to turn their backs on God. God judged Assyria because of her pride. She was driven out of her land because of her wicked pride and arrogance. The most terrible of nations cut her down and chopped off her branches. She lay broken beside the great river of God's blessing. Instead of receiving that blessing with thanksgiving, she had chosen to become proud and arrogant. This resulted in her downfall. The nations who had admired her left her side and went elsewhere. She was alone in her death. Verse 14 tells us that the nations who saw her defeat would never boast of their own prosperity. They would learn the lesson God was trying to teach them about pride and arrogance through Assyria.

If these things happened to the great nation of Assyria, could they not also happen to Egypt? Nations would tremble because of the fall of Egypt. On the day of her judgment, God would hold back the river so that it would no longer bring its blessing to the land of Egypt. The nation of Egypt would be brought down to the grave or hell (NKJV). Egypt would join other fallen nations in the pit. Eden and Lebanon were in that pit. Though not as powerful as Egypt, they were now equal in death. As great as she once was, Egypt would soon lie barren and desolate. The great Pharaoh would be humbled and his nation brought down.

How easy it is to boast in our prosperity and success. What do we ultimately have to boast in? All our greatness could disappear in an instant. All we have, we owe to God. In my few short years on this earth, I have seen great churches being reduced to boxing rings where believers throw their punches at each other. I have seen the strength of people being reduced to nothing by sickness and old age. I have seen friends with secure financial futures lose everything and have to start all over again late in their lives. I've seen the death of youth in the prime of life. My limited experience on this earth tells me that I can boast of nothing, because by tomorrow it may all be gone. How arrogant it is to boast of our security and strength! May God teach us the lesson Egypt needed to learn, before it is too late.

For Consideration:

- What things do you tend to take for granted in this life? How quickly could these things be taken from you? What guarantee do we have of anything in this life?

- What does our boasting really indicate about who we think is in control?

- Why do you think God takes pride so seriously?

For Prayer:

- Thank God for the many blessings he has given you in life.

- Commit these blessings into his hands. Tell God you are willing to let him do with them what he desires.

- Ask God for forgiveness for the times when you have taken these blessings for granted.

- Thank him that he alone is worthy of our confidence. Praise him that in him alone we are secure.

33
Egypt and Her Friends

Read Ezekiel 32

Egypt was compared here to a young lion among the nations, full of strength and vigor (verse 2). She was at the prime of life. She was also compared to a great sea monster, troubling and muddying the waters of the Nile River. She seemed to be so sure of herself. She was powerful and strong and inspired fear and awe among the nations. What could bring her down?

Ezekiel told her that God would cast his net over her (verse 3). A great company of people would come against her and she would be drawn up out of the Nile River. The company of people that God would use would be the Babylonians. This great sea monster would be left on the dry land, cast into an open field. As powerful as she was, she would now become food for the birds of the heavens and the beasts of the earth (verse 4). Her flesh would be spread over the mountains and the valleys (verse 5). Her blood would water the land. The mountains and the river beds would overflow with her blood (verse 6). The sky would be darkened and the nation itself plunged into darkness on that terrible day of God's judgment (verses 7–8). This would not be the first time that such things had taken place in the land of Egypt. In the days of Moses the land was filled with the decaying corpses of the creatures of the sea. Their rivers were filled with blood and the land was plunged into darkness. Their own history told the story of a similar judgment. We have the picture here of a land filled with desolation. Egypt was to fall in the prime of her life. Her greatness would not keep God from judging her. As big as she was, she was no match for the God of Israel.

Notice the response of the surrounding nations to her fall. God would use Egypt as an example to the rest of the world. The hearts of the nations would be troubled because of her fall. Even the nations she did not know would tremble (verse 9). The fall of Egypt would have such an impact on the world that the nations would be brought to their knees in terror, wondering if they were next. Her judgment would speak to the world.

As a nation, Egypt would experience the terror of the hand of God on her. That terror would come in the form of the nation of Babylon (verse 11). This nation had the reputation of being the most terrible of nations (verse 12). Babylon would plunder the wealth of Egypt and destroy its multitudes of people (verse 12). So great would be the fall of Egypt that even the animals of the land would be destroyed (verse 13). No longer would their feet muddy the water of Egypt. The once prosperous nation would be brought low. She would be destitute and barren. When this happened, the world would know the power and holiness of the God of Israel (verse 15).

As he did in chapter 31, God reminded Egypt of the nations before her that had fallen in a similar way. Verses 18–32 speak of some of these nations. Verse 18 explained that they would be cast into the "pit." This pit referred at least to the grave, if not to hell itself. It was a place of no return. Egypt's destiny was with the uncircumcised Gentile nations who had fallen before her. Egypt would join the other nations in the pit of hades where she would remain (verse 21).

Assyria was already in that pit (verse 22). Verses 22 and 23 paint a picture of desolation and darkness for Assyria. She had been a nation that had "spread terror in the land of the living." Assyria was like a graveyard in the pit of hell. The nation of Elam was also there in her grave. She too had caused terror in the land of the living. Therefore, she bore the shame of those who go to the pit of eternal destruction (verse 24). Meshech and Tubal were also among the fallen. They went into hell with all their cruel weapons of war (verse 27 NKJV). Because they had caused terror in the land of the living, they would pay the price in their death. Edom with her kings, despite their military might, was broken and now would be in the company of uncircumcised despisers of God. The Sidonians as well found their company with the most evil nations of the earth. All of these nations would bear the shame of their actions against the land of the living. There in the pit were the greatest and most powerful nations on the earth. They had despised God and his Word and had gone their own way. Then they had paid the price of God's wrath. Now it was Pharaoh's turn to join his fellow evil companions (verse 32).

Here in this chapter we catch a brief glimpse of the pit of hell itself. More and more people are joining this group each day. One by one the company of those who have turned their backs on God in this life is increasing. The story of Egypt's demise is here for our instruction. God is trying to communicate to us the importance of being made right with him right now. The day is coming when we too will have to stand before this same God and be judged. Will you be ready for that day? Would our nation be ready to face God on that day? What will we have to answer for in our day of judgment?

As great as she was, her end would come. Egypt would not be spared from the wrath of God. She would be called on to render an account for her actions. She had been living as though that day would never come. God reminded her that it would indeed come.

How about you? There will be a day of accounting for you too. You do not know when that will be, but for many of us it will not be far away. At best, we only have a few years on this earth. We will then be called before our Creator and Judge. Be assured that this day is coming. Like Egypt, you will not escape it. Are you ready?

For Consideration:

- What things make us feel secure in our day? Where does our only real security come from?

- What do you think it would take for our nation to awaken to the reality of a coming judgment?

- What will you have to answer for on the day of judgment?

- What do we learn here about the judgment of the Lord God?

- Are you ready for the return of the Lord?

For Prayer:

- Ask God to help you to get your priorities right. Ask him to help you see how temporary this life is.

- Ask God to reveal to you any areas of sin in your life that need to be dealt with. Ask him to forgive and heal you of these sins.

- Ask God to give you a greater boldness to share his message of a coming judgment with those who need to hear it.

34

Heed the Watchman

Read Ezekiel 33

H ave you ever had the experience of telling someone something they could not believe? Maybe it was something important or urgent, but they thought you were joking. This can be a frustrating experience. If you have ever experienced this, you may be able to sense in a small way what Ezekiel must have felt when he spoke to his people about God's coming judgment and they turned away in unbelief.

We can see from this chapter that the prophet Ezekiel was called to be a watchman over the house of Israel. God explained Ezekiel's responsibility as a spiritual guard. He was to be always on the alert. When he saw the sword of God's judgment coming against the land of Israel, he was to immediately warn the people in the city. If he warned them and they did not listen, they would die because of their sin. The watchman would not be accountable for what happened to those who refused to listen. If, however, he saw the danger approaching and refused to warn the people, he would be accountable for their deaths. Their blood would be on his hands.

It was not the task of the watchman to act as judge. He could not say to himself: "These people deserve this coming judgment, so I will not alert them." He was not to judge their worthiness or unworthiness to hear God's warning—he was simply to warn them. All men and women are to be told of God's judgment on sin. All people must be given the choice either to heed God's message and repent for their sins or to refuse the word of the watchman. God does not send us only to those he knows will accept wisdom, he sends us also to those who he knows will never chose to obey.

As a prophet, Ezekiel was to speak the words the Lord gave him (see verse 7). Ezekiel was to relay that message to God's people. God has always used his servants to communicate to his people. God gifts and qualifies his people in particular ministries. Each of us has a role to play. Ezekiel's role was to hear God and communicate God's Word to his people. What is your role?

Notice in verse 10 what the people were saying: "Our offenses and sins weigh us down, and we are wasting away because of them. How then can we live?" The Israelites saw God's judgment coming and reasoned that their condition was hopeless. Their sins were crushing them and bringing them to despair. They feared for their lives. Their question is not unlike the question of the jailer who asked Paul what he could do to be saved (Acts 16:30). How we need to come to this point in our society today. How we need to hear people cry out: "How can we live any longer with the weight of our sin?" Only when we understand our need can we truly see the answer God has provided for that need.

God reminded those who cried out in despair because of their sin that he did not take pleasure in the death of the wicked (verse 11). He preferred to see the wicked turn from their wickedness and live. He pleaded with those who grieved for their sin to return to him. "Why should you die?" he asked. There was no reason to perish. A way of escape was open for them. Through repentance they could experience the forgiveness of God. If right then they had turned from their evil ways, he would have accepted them without a moment's hesitation. He did not delight in punishing them. He wanted to pardon them. He was more willing to pardon them than they were to turn from their evil and receive that pardon. They did not have to die because of their sins. Right here in the Old Testament we see God calling the sinner to himself. Through repentance they could have received pardon and life. God's grace was as real in the pages of the Old Testament as it is in the New Testament. This God has never changed. If you have never done so, turn to him right now. He longs to forgive. You do not have to perish.

In verses 12–20 God addressed a misconception that the people of Ezekiel's day had about salvation. They seemed to believe that every good deed they did was credited to some heavenly bank account. When they did evil, they withdrew from this account. When they did something good, they made a deposit in their account. They believed that God would continue to forgive them as long as they did not overdraw their accounts. As long as their deposits were greater than their withdrawals, they would have the approval of God. This is not unlike what many people believe today. What did God say about this teaching here in these verses?

In verses 12–16 the Lord told them that the righteousness of the righteous would not save them in the day they fell into sin, and the wickedness of the wicked would not be held against them in the day they repented (verse 12). What was God saying here? He was telling them that there were no heavenly bank accounts with credits and debits. When righteous Israelites turned their backs on God and did evil things, they would die in the judgment that the Lord was bringing on their land (verse 13). God would not overlook their wickedness just because they had lived righteously in the past. If they were guilty before God, they would have to answer to God for their behavior. On the other hand, even the worst sinners could decide to turn from their wickedness and begin to live righteously. This is what God hoped for (see verse 11). In this case, God would spare their lives in his judgment on the land.

Notice in verses 17–20 that the people of Ezekiel's day found this teaching difficult to accept. "The way of the Lord is not just," they said (verse 17). They refused to take responsibility for the judgment of God on their land. They blamed God alone for all the death and destruction. Their faulty thinking may have been something like this: "Do you mean to tell me that all the good things that I have done will not cancel out the bad things? That is not fair. Shouldn't my good deeds count for something?" God made it clear here in this section that all the good they did would amount to nothing if they were not right with him by turning from their wicked ways and seeking his forgiveness.

How important it is that we get this message. God is not interested in how many good things you have done. He is interested in whether you have been forgiven and are living righteously. You cannot trust in your good deeds. Your only hope can be found in the forgiveness that God offers freely to all who will repent and come to him. You cannot depend on your own efforts. You must cast yourself totally upon the Lord and the forgiveness he freely offers you.

In verse 21 a messenger came to Ezekiel to tell him about the captivity of the city of Jerusalem. Verse 22 tells us that God's hand had been on the prophet the night before this messenger came. We are not told how God's hand was on him, but he obviously knew that something was about to happen. When Ezekiel heard that the city of Jerusalem had been taken, his mouth was opened to speak to the people of God. Verse 22 tells us that he was no longer mute. Obviously, God had kept him from speaking to his people until his judgment on them had been executed. This is in direct fulfillment of the Word of God to him in Ezekiel 24:26–27: "On that day a fugitive will come to tell you the news. At that time your mouth will be opened; you will speak with him and will no longer be silent. So you will be a sign to them, and they will know that I am the LORD."

Verse 23 calls our attention to the people who remained in the ruins of Israel. It appears that these are the people who survived the fall of Jerusalem and were not taken captive by the Babylonians. For the most part, they were poor and unskilled. They were left behind because they were of no practical use to the king of Babylon. Notice that in their pride, they claimed that they had inherited the land their brothers had been banished from. Did they believe that somehow because they had not been taken into exile that they were better than their brothers? God wanted to set the record straight in these verses. He reminded them of their sin as well. He reminded them of how they had been eating the blood of animals and defiling their neighbors' wives. They too would perish by the sword. The land they claimed had been given to them as an inheritance would be given to the wild beasts (verse 27). Those who survived the sword would die of pestilence. The whole land would be made desolate because of their sin.

How easy it is to judge! Sometimes we look down on others and fail to see our own sin. This was what these people were guilty of in their day. Have you ever found yourself looking down on others in a similar way?

Notice that while the people of Ezekiel's day were religious, they were not really interested in what he had to say. They were not ready to seek God with all their heart. In verse 30 we see that these people understood Ezekiel to be a prophet of God. They even invited their brothers and sisters to come and hear him preach. They came and sat down before him to listen to what he had to say. They listened to Ezekiel as they listened to a gifted musician. They listened and maybe even repeated the words among themselves. They talked about the message they heard from the prophet, but they did not do what he said. They were entertained, but they had no intention of putting into practice the words they heard. How many churches are there like this in our day? People come to hear the Word and sing the choruses, but they have no real intention of repenting of their sins.

When you hear the words of the sermon on Sunday morning, do you sneak a peek at your neighbor to see if he is listening to what the preacher is saying but fail to see its application in your life? When you sing your favorite hymn, do you hear the words speak to you and your need of making things right with God? Are you even aware of the words you are singing? God sends his watchmen to us on many occasions. How often, however, have we failed to heed their warnings? We hear the words. They are like a beautiful song. We enjoy the feeling they give us, but it never goes beyond that level.

As you read this commentary, you may enjoy learning more about the prophet Ezekiel, but are you hearing the voice of the watchman? He is warning you of a coming danger. He is calling you to turn from your sins and live. Do you hear him? Will you take his words seriously? Will you be like the people of Israel who did not take the prophet seriously? Will you heed the watchman and live?

For Consideration:

- Has God called you to be a watchman today? What is your particular role?

- What do we learn here about salvation? What is the teaching of Ezekiel regarding salvation by good works?

- What is the difference between listening to the watchman and doing something about what he says?

For Prayer:

- Ask God to help you hear him and know his leading.

- Ask him to open up your eyes each day to see opportunities to share his love.

- Is there someone you believe needs to be warned of coming judgment? Take a moment to bring this person before the Lord in prayer.

- Ask God to forgive you for the times that you did not take him and his Word seriously.

35
Shepherds and Sheep

Read Ezekiel 34

Have you ever been disappointed in a spiritual leader? Has another believer ever hurt you? These problems are all too common in our day. One of the major problems with the nation of Israel was that her leaders were not committed to caring for the people. There were also people among them who did not seek unity. God compared the leaders of the nation to shepherds and the people to sheep. Let's look at what was taking place in the land.

The shepherds were concerned only for themselves (verse 2). They took advantage of the sheep. They ate their curds (NIV), clothed themselves with their wool, and killed the choicest of the flock for their own food (verse 3). They took from the flock but did not take care of it. They did not strengthen the weak. They did not heal the sick. They did not care for the injured. They did not bring back the straying. They did not bother to search for the lost. They ruled over them harshly. Obviously, their concern was not for the sheep but for themselves.

The result of this lack of care was that the sheep were scattered. They left the fold, and no one came to their rescue. They wandered dangerously far away and were easy prey for the wild beasts. The shepherds did nothing to return them to the fold or rescue them from their enemies. Is this happening in the churches of our land today? Are there pastors and spiritual leaders in our churches today who serve only for what they can get themselves? What should we think when pastors refuse positions simply because the money and benefits are not what they want? Why is it that the larger and more prestigious churches seem to be able to find full-time workers, while the low-salaried, rural churches struggle to find anyone to come to their aid? Aren't churches all across our nation filled with people who have not grown spiritually for years? There are many who do not know the Lord but preach behind the pulpits of our churches. How can they bind up the broken with the message of salvation in Jesus when they themselves have never accepted this message? Churchgoers all across our world are on a road heading straight to an eternity without Jesus. Their spiritual leaders do nothing to warn them. They content themselves with maintaining a good reputation in the church and community. They do not want to rock the boat. The result is starving and scattered sheep. What Ezekiel said here about these shepherds applies equally to our churches today. May God help us to listen carefully to his warning.

The Lord was angry with these shepherds. In verse 10 God clearly told them that he was "against the shepherds." God would hold them accountable for their actions. He would not allow them to continue in their role as shepherds. He cared too much for his sheep to let them be destroyed by the shepherds. We cannot take this verse lightly. God was "against" these shepherds. There is a tremendous responsibility that comes with being a shepherd of God's people. If the sheep under your pastoral care are not growing, it is your responsibility to see that they do. To neglect your responsibility or to exercise your role as pastor purely for selfish motives is to invite the wrath of God. You have in your hands the care of a people whom God dearly loves. We dare not neglect such an awesome task. In Ezekiel 34 the spiritual and political leaders of God's people had been found guilty before God of neglecting the sheep.

What was the solution to this problem? God himself would care for his sheep. He would take the sheep from the hands of those who had been neglecting and misleading them. He would search for those who had been scattered and bring them back to the fold (verses 11–12). He would rescue them and bring them back to their homeland (verses 12–13). Once again they would graze in rich pastures (verse 14). The sick would be healed. The weak would be strengthened (verse 16). What a tremendous promise this is!

Scattered throughout the churches of our land and among those who content themselves with nominal Christianity and tradition are those who truly belong to the Lord. Even though they belong to him, they are spiritually starving. They are not hearing the message of the gospel in their churches. They are not encouraged to step out in their faith. Some do not even know that there is much more to the faith they profess than what they are presently experiencing. I have seen many of these people. Over the last few years I have had the privilege of ministering to some of them. I have seen them come to life under the clear teaching of the Scriptures. I have seen them flower and produce fruit. God has not abandoned them. He has sought them out because he loved them. This is what was happening in this passage.

It should be noted here that the immediate fulfilment of this prophecy would take place when the people of God returned from their land of exile. Their spiritual leaders had not led them in the way of truth. They had led them into idol worship and pagan practices. God's people were scattered all over the globe because of their sins. God would not abandon them. He would return them to their land.

In verses 17–22 we find that it was not only the shepherds who had been causing problems for God's people. Among the flock were sheep that trampled the pasture and muddied the clear water, forcing the other sheep to eat what they had trampled down and drink what they had muddied (verse 19). These sheep shoved and butted the weakest of the flock with their horns (verse 21). The weaker sheep were scattered because of them.

You do not have to go very far to find this type of overbearing sheep. It seems that every church has a few bad sheep. These people are proud. They want their own way. Some of them are very disagreeable. They seem to rub people the wrong way. They say things that cause a stir among the flock. In their presence the flock is agitated and tense. Some want recognition. They want to have others look up to them. They can be very bitter and domineering. God is aware of the presence of this type of sheep in the flock. The day is coming when they will be judged.

Things were not easy for God's people. Their shepherds had failed them. They were abused by fellow believers. They were broken and crushed. God would not abandon them, however. He would raise up his servant David to lead them (verse 23). Who was this servant? Was it not the Lord Jesus himself, the son of David? The Lord Jesus, as the Good Shepherd, would protect his sheep (verse 25). With him as their shepherd, they would live in peace (verse 25). Under his leadership they would be richly blessed. Showers would come in their season (verse 26). Their trees would yield their fruit (verse 27). The people would live in security (verse 27). No longer would they be plundered by the nations. No one would make them afraid because God himself would be their shepherd (verse 28).

What a wonderful promise! Your brothers and sisters may have mistreated you. Your spiritual leaders may have neglected you in your time of spiritual need. Jesus will never let you down. He will always be there for you. You can trust him fully. When everyone else has disappointed you, he will be there to pick you up. He loves you too much to abandon you. Are you willing to let him feed you? Will you let him be your guide? Will you listen to him and follow his leading? He will care for you. Those of us who have submitted ourselves to the Lord Jesus know the blessings of his lordship in our lives. In him we are strong. In him no foe can destroy us. We are secure in his grace. His care is perfect. There is no wound he cannot heal. There is no pain he cannot comfort. In him we are truly blessed. He is indeed the Good Shepherd.

God condemned the leaders of Israel because they did not care for the sheep. He condemned the bad sheep in the fold because they agitated the fold and drove away weaker sheep. Maybe you can identify with what Ezekiel was saying here. Maybe you have experienced the neglect and abuse of spiritual authority in your church. Maybe you have been butted by the horn of a bad sheep. As long as we look to people, we will be disappointed. May I draw your attention to the Great Shepherd? Unlike your brothers and sisters, he will never let you down. In him you will always be loved and protected. The Lord Jesus is God himself, the Great Shepherd of the sheep. In your turmoil turn your eyes to him. You will not be disappointed.

For Consideration:

- Why do you suppose there are shepherds who do not shepherd the sheep today? What is their motivation in ministry?

- Have you met individuals in your church who seem to create disharmony? What is the warning of God to them here in this passage?

- What does this passage teach us about the love and care of the Lord God for his sheep?

- What do we learn here about the awesome responsibility that is put on the shoulders of spiritual leaders to care for God's sheep? Are you a spiritual leader? What challenge does this passage bring to you?

- What keeps believers in churches where the gospel is not being preached?

For Prayer:

- Ask God to bless your pastor in his ministry. Ask God to help him to serve with a true and pure heart.

- Do you know believers who have been part of a church for years but have never grown? Take a moment to bring them before the Lord in prayer.

- Pray for those shepherds in your community who have not been shepherding the sheep. Ask God to help them to know him and take their responsibility seriously.

36

Old Grudges

Read Ezekiel 35

Have you ever kept a grudge? Maybe you were hurt many years ago by someone, and you have never been able to forgive that person. This is what took place in chapter 35 of Ezekiel. God spoke here to the inhabitants of Mount Seir. A quick look at Deuteronomy 2:12 will show us that the inhabitants of this region were the descendants of Esau: "Horites used to live in Seir, but the descendants of Esau drove them out. They destroyed the Horites from before them and settled in their place, just as Israel did in the land the LORD gave them as their possession." The descendants of Esau were also known as the Edomites. Genesis 36:1 tells us: "This is the account of Esau (that is, Edom)."

Our passage tells us that God was angry with the Edomites. He would make their land a desolate waste and their towns would be ruined (verse 4). Why was God angry with the Edomites? The Bible tells us that the Edomites "harbored an ancient hostility" (verse 5). The KJV says that they had a "perpetual hatred" in their hearts. The context tells us that this hatred was directed toward the children of Israel. What was the source of this perpetual hatred between the Edomites and the people of Israel and Judah? Genesis 27:41 gives us the answer: "Esau held a grudge against Jacob because of the blessing his father had given him. He said to himself, 'The days of mourning for my father are near; then I will kill my brother Jacob.'"

Jacob had stolen Esau's birthright. After that Jacob fled, and the two brothers were separated because of the hatred of Esau toward his brother Jacob. This bitterness continued throughout the years. Hundreds of years had passed since this event, and yet the two nations had still not resolved their differences. Edom continued to cultivate the old hostility between Jacob and Esau.

What was the result of this "ancient hostility"? What happens when we harbor ill feelings in our soul toward another? Let's look at the result of this bitterness.

Judgment and Desolation

First, notice that Edom brought the judgment of God on herself and her land. Their land would become a barren wasteland (verse 7). Her mountains would be filled with the bodies of the slain (verse 8). Her towns would be uninhabited (verse 9). We see here a picture of brokenness and despair. What God promised would happen to Edom will happen to anyone who repeats Edom's errors. When we hold a grudge against our brother or sister, we bring desolation to our own souls. We cut ourselves off from fellowship with God's children and with God himself. The natural result of this is barrenness in our spiritual and emotional lives.

Broken Fellowship with Brothers and Sisters

Second, we see in this passage that bitterness destroyed

the relationship between Edom and Israel. Edom rejoiced here over the destruction of Jerusalem (verse 15). She cared nothing for Israel's pain and suffering. Her bitter spirit had stripped her of compassion for her brothers and sisters. She could not feel for them. When enemies invaded Israel, she stood on the sidelines cheering them on. Listen to what the Psalmist says in Psalm 137:7: "Remember, O LORD, what the Edomites did on the day Jerusalem fell. 'Tear it down,' they cried, 'tear it down to its foundations!'"

We understand from Ezekiel that Edom had nothing but evil to say about God's people: "Then you will know that I the LORD have heard all the contemptible things you have said against the mountains of Israel. You said, 'They have been laid waste and have been given over to us to devour'" (verse 12).

Edom claimed that the lands of Israel and Judah were rightfully hers (verse 10). In saying this she was going back to her stolen birthright and blessing. The Edomites felt that they were the rightful owner of the land that God had given to Israel because they were the rightful owners of the blessing and birthright that Jacob had stolen from his twin brother, Esau. Israel's prosperity was a constant reminder of these stolen blessings.

The hatred and jealousy in the heart of Edom caused her to lash out against Israel, destroying any possibility of relationship between the two nations. Harboring old grudges will only serve as a barrier to restored relationships with our brother or sister. Only when we deal with the bitterness can relationships be restored.

Broken Fellowship with God

Third, notice that the harboring of grudges also destroys our relationship with God. God was against Edom because of her "perpetual hatred." Verse 6 tells us that God would pursue her to shed her blood. Edom developed a bad attitude, not only toward the Israelites but also toward God who so richly blessed them. She resented the fact that God had taken Israel's side in this ancient hostility. She began to openly show her disapproval. Verse 13 tells us that Edom boasted against God and spoke against him "without restraint."

There is a very intimate relationship between God and his people. To hurt a child of God is to hurt God himself. Matthew 25:40 puts it this way: "The King will reply, 'I tell you the truth, whatever you did for one of the least of these brothers of mine, you did for me.'" You cannot separate your relationship with others from your relationship with their Heavenly Father. When you cultivate a bad attitude toward the people of God, you cultivate that same attitude toward God. What we do to the least of his children, he considers that we are doing it to him. This destroys our relationship with God. You can only get as close to God as you are to his children. You cannot love God if you do not love his children. Edom's bitterness toward the children of God broke their relationship with God himself.

Are you in this situation today? Do you harbor bitterness against a brother or sister in Christ? Ultimately, we hurt only ourselves in holding grudges against others. Only by extending forgiveness and seeking reconciliation can we know spiritual peace and prosperity in our own lives.

For Consideration:

• Have you ever found yourself holding a grudge against a fellow human being? What was the result of this in your life spiritually and emotionally?

• Why is it so hard to seek reconciliation? What keeps us from seeking reconciliation?

• Do you have trouble forgiving a certain person? Who is it?

For Prayer:

- Ask the Lord to reveal to you any personal bitterness that you may be harboring in your heart against a brother or sister.

- Ask God to bring healing in your life from this bitterness.

- Ask him to fill your life with forgiveness for those who have offended you.

37

The Coming Revival

Read Ezekiel 36

All of us have had the experience of having to clean up a big mess. Junk has a tendency to accumulate over the years. It clutters up our houses and leaves little room for the things we really need. From time to time we feel the need to do a good cleaning. What a joy it is to get rid of the clutter in our homes! From time to time the clutter accumulates as well in the lives of the people of God. God is forced to do something about it.

In this chapter attention was focused on the mountains of Israel. These mountains had been deserted (verse 3). They were barren because the people of God had lost their land. Israel's enemies had left her land abandoned. They openly boasted that these mountains were now theirs (verse 2). Israel's adversaries were openly slandering her (verse 3).

Notice God's response when he saw the enemies rejoice because of the downfall of his people (verse 5). These were his children they were mocking. He was jealous for them (verse 6). Like any good father, he would not sit idly by while his children suffered rebuke. He was going to lift up his hand against his children's enemies (verse 7). God promised that these barren mountains of Israel would again produce fruit (verse 8). He would again bless his people. It is true that God's people were being punished for their sins, but they were his children. He still loved them. He had a very bright future in store for them. Once again Israel's uncultivated lands would be plowed and sown (verse 9). Her towns would be rebuilt and inhabited as before (verse 10). They would again become a numerous people (verse 11). Israel would regain her former glory and prosper more than she had in the past (verse 11). Never again would the mountains be deprived of inhabitants (verse 12). People said that the mountains of Israel had devoured their own people (verse 13). No longer would they be able to say that. Israel's enemies would no longer scorn her (verse 15).

It is important to mention here that it was not because Israel deserved these blessings that God was going to respond favorably toward her. She was like a woman in her monthly impurity (verse 17). She was impure. Because of her corruption, God had dispersed her among the nations (verse 19). She had been exiled because of her sin (verse 19). Even in her exile, Israel had profaned the name of the Lord by her evil practices (verse 20). Her disobedience to God was the subject of much talk among the nations (verse 20).

It was not because she merited God's favor that she was to be blessed. It was because God's holy name was being profaned that God would draw her back to himself (verse 22). Because Israel was in exile, the nations would conclude that Israel's God was not powerful enough to keep her in his land. For the sake of his great name, he would do a future work among his people.

What was this work that God was going to do? He would gather them from their exile and sprinkle clean water on them to cleanse them from their sin (verse 25). He would give them a new heart and put a new spirit within them (verse 25). He would remove the old heart of stone and rebellion (verse 26). He would give them his Spirit. His Spirit would move them to obedience (verse 27). They would truly become God's people, not only in name but also in deed (verse 28). They would be saved from their uncleanness (verse 29). Once again they would be blessed (verse 30). In that day they would remember their evil ways and loathe themselves for having stooped so low (verse 31). Noticed here that it was not for them that God would do this work but, rather, for the sake of his holy name (verse 32).

What would be the result of this revival in the land? Notice four things in this passage. First, their desolate land would become a Garden of Eden (verse 35). The blessing of the Lord would be poured out on the land. His presence would be obvious. When God comes in revival, barrenness departs. We cannot help but look at our world today and see the spiritual desolation and barrenness that abounds. When God pours out his Spirit in revival, the barren wilderness is always watered and begins to bring forth fruit. The Word of the Lord is once more respected and the name of the Lord is honored.

The second result of this revival would be that the nations would know that Israel's God was the true God (verse 36). When God gave them a new heart and a new spirit, the nations would see the difference in the lives of his people. When God poured out his Spirit on the church at Pentecost, the world could not help but notice the difference. When Christians live in the power of the Spirit of God, others begin to bow the knee before their God.

Third, notice in verse 37 that God promised to increase the house of Israel "like a flock." In an age of declining church membership and waning interest in spiritual matters, how we need such a move of God's Spirit today.

Fourth, notice that Israel would bow the knee before God (verse 38). They would see his powerful work among them and fall down in worship and adoration. He would be glorified among his people. They would know him to be God. Although they had been unfaithful to their God, he would move in power and restore them to a right relationship with him.

Our present age is in need of this kind of revival promised to the house of Israel. We seek not a revival for ourselves—we seek it for the glory of God's holy name. His name is being profaned in our workplaces as people take it in vain. His name is being profaned in our country as policies are being made that directly contradict the teaching of the Word of God. His name is being profaned in our schools as young people live in immorality, abusing alcohol and drugs. His name is being profaned on our televisions and in our music. His name is being profaned in our business world as people step on others for their own advancement. His name is being profaned in our churches as believers come together to worship without ever dealing with the sin that separates them one from another. His name is being profaned from our pulpits as preachers preach a word that is not from the Lord. His name is being profaned in our own lives as we fail to live fully unto him. For the glory of the holy name of God, we need to cry out for the kind of revival promised to Israel. Can we sit idly by as our society blasphemes the name of our God? Won't you cry out today that God would remove the old stony hearts and replace them with hearts of flesh?

For Consideration:

- What evidence is there in our present society that we need to experience the kind of revival spoken of here in this chapter?

- What would you expect to see changed by this great revival in our midst?

- Is there evidence of a need of revival in your own personal life? Be specific.

- What is the primary purpose of revival here according to Ezekiel?

For Prayer:

- Ask God to bring about this revival in our society.

- Ask him to give you personally this heart for revival in your own life.

38

An Army of Dried Bones

Read Ezekiel 37

The setting is a valley. Ezekiel had been taken there in a vision from the Lord. God walked him through the valley in his vision. There were bones scattered over the ground. These bones were very dry. Obviously, they had been there for a long time. It was as though some great battle had taken place in this valley. Ezekiel was seeing the bodies of those who had died in this great battle.

As Ezekiel took in the scene before him, he heard the Lord asking him if these bones could live again. Ezekiel told God that only he could decide whether these bones could live again. Humanly speaking, it was not possible, but with God anything was possible.

God then asked the prophet to prophesy to the bones. Ezekiel obeyed the Lord and prophesied. We are not told how he did this or what he said. God obviously gave him the words he needed to speak. When he finished speaking, he heard a sound rising up from the floor of the valley. It was a rattling sound. As he looked around him, he saw the bones beginning to move. It was as if a skilled workman, invisible to the human eye, was putting these bones together. Piece by piece they came together. When each bone had found its correct place, Ezekiel saw tendons and flesh appear on the dry skeletons. Soon these bodies were covered with skin. The corpses lay silent on the ground. While their bodies had been restored, there was still no life in them. Like many churches of our day they had an outward form, but there was no life in them.

Then the LORD told Ezekiel to speak "to the breath" and say: "Come from the four winds, O breath, and breathe into these slain, that they may live" (verse 9). Ezekiel obeyed. He heard the wind blow into the valley. Life came with the wind and the slain rose to their feet very much alive. Ezekiel looked around and saw a very impressive army.

What was this vision about? God explained to the prophet that the bones were his people, Israel. They had been cut off. They were without hope. God would restore them, however. He would give them back their land. He would bring them back from their exile and cause them to enjoy the land he had promised their forefathers. God would not only return them to their land, but his wind would give them spiritual life (verse 14). His Spirit would come upon them in refreshing revival power. When everything seemed to be lost, God moved and hope was restored.

God promised that he would open up their graves and restore life. How we need to see this in our day! Once again we need to see the graves of spiritually dead believers opened up and these individuals restored to new life in Christ. Once again we need to see the churches of our age renewed with new life from above so that they rise from their spiritual apathy and indifference to serve and glorify their Lord and Savior.

After this God commanded Ezekiel to take two sticks and write on them (verse 16). On the first stick he was to write: "For Judah and for the children of Israel his companions"

(KJV) On the second stick these words were to be recorded: "For Joseph, the stick of Ephraim, and for all the house of Israel his companions" (KJV). What are we to make of this? Many years before this, the people of God had been divided into two nations: Israel and Judah. These sticks represented these nations. Ezekiel was to take the two sticks and join them in his hands, representing the fact that once again they would be one nation. No longer would they be divided. This took place upon their return from exile. They returned as one nation. The old hostilities were cast aside.

Not only were these dead bones given new life, they would also live together in unity. When they returned they would be united under one king (verse 22). They would be cleansed of their sin and no longer would they defile themselves with their idols (verse 23). The king who would rule over them is described here as being "my servant David." Who is this king? Obviously, it is not King David who had died many years before this. This king would, however, come from the line of David. The Lord Jesus Christ is from the line of David. He himself would be their new king. According to verse 24, he would lead his people in obedience to the commands of God. He would establish a new covenant with them. He would be their king forever more. No other king but Jesus could fulfill this prophecy. He alone could reign over his people eternally. What a bright hope was theirs as they looked forward to the coming of this great king to rule over them!

The immediate fulfillment of this prophecy came to pass when God's people returned from exile and settled back in their land. Here they were given new life. They were united together as one nation, just as God had promised through Ezekiel. The problem, however, arises when we see the response of the Jews toward their new king, the Lord Jesus. Our passage tells us that they would be careful to observe his laws. This is not what we see, however, when the Lord

Jesus came to earth. The Jews rejected him as their king. It would seem, therefore, that the Lord has still a great work to accomplish in the lives of his people. Will he cause a great revival to take place among the Jews? Will they, as a people, turn to the Lord Jesus and accept him as their Messiah? We await this ultimate fulfillment.

What we need to understand here, however, is that though the Jews generally rejected the Lord Jesus as their Messiah, it was from them that the New Testament church sprang. We cannot forget that the disciples of our Lord Jesus were Jews. These men took the message of Jesus to the world. It was God's heart to reach out through his people to the ends of the earth: "Then the nations will know that I the LORD make Israel holy, when my sanctuary is among them forever" (verse 28).

God promised here to place his "sanctuary" among the nations. In the Old Testament context, this term referred to the place God's presence resided (Psalm 102:19; Leviticus 4:6) When God told Ezekiel that his sanctuary would dwell forever with his people, God was telling him that his presence would be with them. This revival would accomplish a third objective: not only would it bring new life to God's people and unite them under one Lord, but it would also move them out in ministry to the ends of the earth.

When the Holy Spirit was poured out on these Jewish disciples of Jesus at Pentecost, three thousand men and women were added to the church in one day. In the days that followed the coming of the Holy Spirit, people were being added daily to the church. When the presence of the Lord came to live among his people, the nations were touched. From that little group of Jewish believers, gathered together in Jerusalem, an international church was born. From these dried-out Jewish bones, God formed a mighty army. That army spread throughout the world with the message of the gospel. It continues to flourish today.

How we need to praise the Lord that he is doing a mighty work on the earth today. From the rebellious nations of Israel and Judah, he raised up an army of believers. Today that mighty army is moving all across the earth. In the history of the church, we have never seen such a spread of the gospel. The message of the gospel of Christ has spread to every country. People from every nationality have turned their hearts and lives over to the lordship of Jesus Christ. From those dried-out bones God has indeed formed a mighty army. He can also use you. He is a life-giving God. You may feel unworthy and helpless, but this passage reminds us that with God all things are possible. Will you trust him and step out in faith?

For Consideration:

- What hope do you find here in this chapter for the future of the church?

- What would be the fruit of this revival that God would bring to Israel? In their lives? In the lives of those around them?

- What does this passage teach us about the possibility of having a form but having no life? What is that life?

- What change has the Spirit of God made in your life?

For Prayer:

- Are there people you know who have "died" to spiritual matters in their life? Take a moment to ask God to breathe life into their dead bones.

- Ask God to bring this renewal to your life and the life of your church.

- Notice that in this renewal that God would bring, relationships would be mended. Is there someone that you have trouble loving? Ask God to bring healing to this relationship.

39

The Destruction of Gog

Read Ezekiel 38

One of the greatest blessings of the Christian life is the knowledge that we are more than conquerors in Christ Jesus. There is no foe that can overcome us. There is no temptation that is too powerful for us to master. This does not mean that we will not have to face obstacles in our lives. Though there will be trials and testing in this life we can be assured that in Christ, we are more than conquerors.

In chapters 38 and 39 Ezekiel was called to prophesy against Gog. Who is Gog? We understand from Ezekiel 38:2 that Gog was a prince of the lands of Magog, Meshech, and Tubal. These regions were located in the present area of Turkey. From Genesis 10:2 we read that Magog, Meshech, and Tubal were the sons of Japheth and grandchildren of Noah.

From verses 4–6 we discover that Gog was a very powerful and influential leader in his day. Mention was made of his great army. This army was equipped with a number of horses and horsemen splendidly armed with swords and shields. What made Gog even more imposing was the fact that he was the leader of a very powerful alliance of nations. Joined with his army were the armies of Persia, Cush, Put, Gomer, and Beth Togarmah. Who would dare to stand against such a foe?

The time was coming, prophesied Ezekiel, when Gog and his alliance of nations would invade a land "recovered from war" (verse 8). The people they would invade were a people who had been gathered from the surrounding nations and brought to the mountains of Israel. This nation was none other than the restored nation of Israel. Like a storm, Gog and his alliance would advance against the people of God (verse 9). Notice here that the inhabitants of this land lived peacefully in unwalled villages (verse 11). Like a bully stealing candy from a little child, Gog and his great army would plunder defenseless Israel. He would attack, plunder, and loot the resettled ruins of Israel (verse 12).

Out of the north, Gog and his alliance of nations would come up against the people of God, like a great cloud covering the land (verse 15–16). We are told that this battle would not take place until the latter days, when the people of God were again resettled in their land (verse 16). While this was not a pleasant future to look forward to, the Lord did bring an encouraging word to his people. When Gog invaded the land of Israel, the anger of God would be aroused. The earth would shake when God rose up in righteous fury (verse 19). All of creation, from the fish of the sea to the birds of the heavens, would tremble in the presence of this God of holy anger. Men and women living on the surface of the earth in those days would also tremble at the presence of this great and awesome God. In the day of his wrath, the mountains would be overturned. The cliffs would fall flat. The walls of the cities would fall to the ground, leaving the inhabitants without defense. On that day, God would summon the sword against Gog (verse 21). Gog had come to destroy, but he himself would be destroyed. The day of God's wrath would be a day of plague and bloodshed. God would open up the gates of heaven and pour down on Gog a deluge of rain, hailstones, and burning sulphur, executing his judgment against him (verse 22).

How are we to understand this prophecy? The apostle John prophesied of a similar event in Revelation 20:7–10. In this passage Satan will be released from his bonds. He will go forth to deceive the nations. He will gather Gog and Magog together and march against the camp of God's people. This is not unlike what is being described for us in Ezekiel. Satan will not be successful. Revelation 20:9 tells us that fire will rain down from heaven on Gog and Magog. Ezekiel spoke of a similar thing when he wrote that God would pour down "torrents of rain, hailstones and burning sulphur" on Gog and his army. Do these two passages refer to the same event?

Is this prophecy yet to be fulfilled? Will the people of God yet see a great persecution? What is this great army that will invade the people of God? When will this take place? While we do not have clear answers to these questions, we can be assured that Satan has not given up. The Bible tells us that he will be unleashed upon this earth in the latter days. When he is unleashed, his battle against the people of God will be cruel. We do not know when or how this will take place. It suffices for us to be warned that it will take place.

What is essential for us to understand in this chapter is that in Christ there is complete victory. Satan will do his best to destroy the work of God. He will attack us and hurl his allies against us. We will be called on to suffer. We must accept the inevitable fact that we are involved in a spiritual warfare. It should not surprise us to see the enemy shoot at us. Some of us will suffer the deadly blows of Satan's arrow in our fight against him. The Christian walk is one of discipline and difficulty. There will be times when the size of the enemy coming toward us will tempt us to be discouraged and lose heart. Ezekiel 38 calls us to persevere. The victory is ours. We can overcome. God will not allow us to be defeated. The world will one day bow at his feet and recognize that he is Lord of all. Praise be to God who gives us the victory through our Lord Jesus Christ (1 Corinthians 15:57). We will overcome. Ezekiel promised victory over Gog and his mighty army. Satan is a defeated foe. May the assurance of victory give us courage to face the battle before us.

For Consideration:

• What encouragement do you take from this particular chapter?

• Why do you suppose God allows this great army to come against his people? Is there a purpose for the trials and difficulties we go through in this life?

For Prayer:

• Take a moment to thank God that he is bigger than anything the enemy can throw against you.

• Can you recall times in your life when you too had to face a foe that was far bigger than you? Take a moment to praise and thank the Lord for the victory he gave you at that time of your life.

40
Why God Sends Trials

Read Ezekiel 39

We have seen how Gog would invade the land of Israel and be destroyed in the process. Here in this chapter Ezekiel continued his prophecy against Gog and her people. Verse 1 tells us that God was against Gog. She had attacked the people of God in their time of peace. Notice here in verse 2 that God himself led this enemy from the north to the nation of Israel. We are given the distinct impression here that God was bringing Gog to attack the land of Israel. Why would God allow his people to be attacked? The following verses shed some light on this question. They also shed some light on the problem of evil and pain in our society today. Let's examine why God allowed Gog to attack his people.

Notice first in verse 3 that while God led Gog to come against his people, he also knocked the sword out of her hands. Gog and all her troops would fall on the mountains of Israel. The birds of prey would feed on their corpses (verse

4). While they lay dying in the open field, God would send a fire to their homelands, destroying them completely (verse 6). God's people would be stretched in their faith. They would have to trust him as the enemy approached. God would bring Israel to the brink of disaster and then break through in victory. God would remain in control.

Even though things around you seem to be falling apart and you are feeling the enemy breathing down your neck, never doubt that God is in control. He knows what he is doing. He knows what you can handle and promises victory to all who trust in him. Notice what the result of this pain would be. In verse 6 Ezekiel tells us that when these things would happen, God's people would know that he was the LORD (the Sovereign One). If we never had a problem, how could we experience the power of God to overcome our problems? God shows us how big he really is by allowing these problems to come our way and then giving us victory over them.

Verse 7 tells us another thing about our difficulties: through them God brings glory to his holy name. When we see the victory of God over sin and pain, our response is one of praise and thanksgiving. When we see how God deals with evil and rebellion, we are moved to obedience and faithfulness. God sometimes allows evil to happen so that through it he can demonstrate his great holiness and hatred of sin. God allowed Gog to attack his people. He showed his people the horrible nature of sin through Gog. Then he showed them his great judgment of that sin. The end result was that God's people had a deeper appreciation of his hatred of sin and his holiness of character.

Verses 9–16 paint a picture of the defeat of Gog. Before us we see the bodies of Gog's army strewn across the land. Their weapons are scattered all around them. So large was the quantity of weapons used against the people of God that they would not have to search for firewood for seven years.

They would simply burn their enemy's weapons of war (verse 9–10). It would take the Israelites seven months to bury the soldiers that perished in that great battle (verse 12). Men would be hired to go throughout the land and search out the dead bodies lying unattended in the fields. When they found a body, they would set up a marker (verse 15). Other men would come behind them and bury the corpses (verse 14). In verses 17–20 the birds of the air and the wild animals of the forest would be called on to assist in this massive clean up operation. They would eat the flesh of the enemies of Israel until they could eat no more. They would drink blood until they were drunk. It would be by this means that the land would be cleansed of its defilement.

What would happen if the Lord were to do a similar search in the churches of our day? Would he find any dying corpses of sin and rebellion? What about your own life? If God were to send his angels to search the hidden recesses of your life, what would he find? The Psalmist cried out to God to search him (Psalms 139:23–24). How we need to have this attitude!

Come, Lord, and search my heart. Dig up those unforgiven hurts and pains. Uncover those unconfessed sins. Reveal to me my wrong attitudes and motives. Show me those things that keep me from experiencing more of you. Come and cleanse me. Come and renew me, however painful that might be.

We see in verses 22–24 another reason for pain and trials. God uses them to discipline us and draw us back to himself. From verse 23 we learn that God sent his people into exile and allowed pain and trials to overwhelm them because of their unfaithfulness. He hid his face from them and gave them into the hands of the enemy. He dealt with them according to their evil ways (verse 24). While we should not always assume that we suffer because of some secret sin, the discipline of God is nonetheless very real.

There are times when God will allow trials and pain to overwhelm us in order to awaken us to the reality of our rebellion. Notice, however, that this discipline does not last forever. After they had borne their shame and learned their lessons, God would again come to them. Once again they would dwell in safety and security. Their enemies would be held back. Again God would reveal his face to them, never to hide it again (verse 29). He would pour out his Spirit on them (verse 29). God's name would be lifted up among his people and his glory would be seen by many nations (verse 27). Their discipline was only for a time. Through their pain, God drew them to himself. They were refined in the fire of his discipline. All this had as its objective to draw his loved ones closer to himself.

For Consideration:

• What are the three reasons for pain discussed here in this chapter? Do you see any practical examples of this in your life?

• We saw that though the Lord allows pain, he still remains in control of that pain. What comfort do you take from this? Can you apply this truth to something you are going through in your life right now?

• How have trials and pain drawn you closer to the Lord Jesus?

For Prayer:

• Take a moment and ask the Lord to search your heart. Ask him to uncover anything that needs to be confessed and made right.

- Ask him for the strength to step out and make these things right.

- Thank him for the trial you are going through right now. Praise him that he is not only in control of this pain but is also using it to bring glory to his name.

41

Ezekiel's Temple

Read Ezekiel 40:1–43:12

I n times of trial, the last thing we think about is looking at all the blessings that the Lord has given us. It is in these moments, however, that we need to lift up our spirits and remember the great promises of God. Nothing will renew our courage more than our hopes of brighter things to come. When we realize that our sufferings are only for a season, we are restored in our efforts to persevere.

In this section the prophet Ezekiel was taken, by means of a vision, to the land of Israel.[1] This vision took place in the twenty-fifth year of the Babylonian captivity, fourteen years after the city was captured. This shows us that Ezekiel was one of the first captives to leave his homeland for Babylon. The Israelites were sent into exile in various stages. Over a period of years, the enemy had been taking God's people captive. In his vision Ezekiel was taken to the top of a mountain. From there, as he looked toward the south, he saw what appeared to be a great city. He was taken to the city where he met a man whose appearance was like bronze (verse 3 NIV) or brass (KJV). This was probably a reference to his brilliance. This man stood by the gate with a linen cord and a measuring rod in his hand (verse 3). Ezekiel was commanded to examine very carefully what the man was about to show him. What he saw he was to tell to the children of Israel (verse 4).

Ezekiel noticed a great temple in this city. All around the temple was a wall. The man with the measuring rod measured the wall. It stood one rod in height and one rod in thickness (that is 3 meters or 9 feet in height and width). This wall was obviously very solid.

To simplify the description of this temple, I have included a diagram. The diagram is not meant to be a perfect architectural plan. It will give us a rough idea, however, of the temple that is described for us in the next few chapters. Let us consider this temple.

Figure 41.1

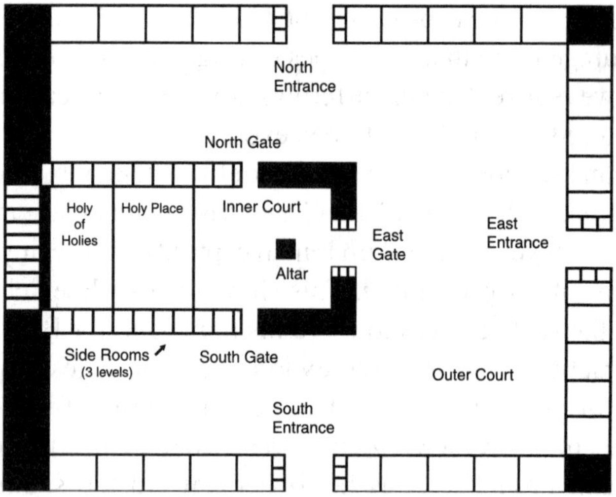

As we have already mentioned, a great wall surrounded the temple (verses 5–6). Ezekiel watched as the man with the rod went to the east entrance to measure the threshold. It measured one rod (3 meters or 9 feet). One could enter into the outer court of the temple area by one of three entrances (east entrance, verse 6; north entrance, verse 20; south entrance, verse 24). Seven steps led up into these entrances (verse 22, 26). Each entrance had three "alcoves for the guards" on each side (verses 7, 10, 21). The alcoves measured one square rod (3 square meters or 9 square feet, verse 6). Ezekiel noticed that there were windows all around.

Ezekiel and his guide entered into the outer court of the temple (verse 17). Ezekiel noticed the rooms built into the walls of the outer court. There were thirty rooms along the walls (verse 17). These chambers were used for storage. This would explain the reason for the three-meter-wide wall, as the rooms were set into the wall. Ezekiel was taken from the east gate (verse 6) to the north gate (verse 20) and finally to the south gate (verse 24). As they moved from gate to gate, Ezekiel noted all the details while the man with the rod calculated the measurements.

After examining the outer court, the two men moved toward the inner court of the temple (verse 28). The inner court measured one hundred cubits long and one hundred cubits wide (approximately 46 meters or 150 feet). This court also had three gates (south, verse 28; east, verse 32; north, verse 35). These inner gateways lined up with the entrances of the outer court. Eight steps led up into the inner court, making it at a higher level than the outer court (verse 31). Ezekiel and his guide moved through the inner courtyard from the south (verse 28) to the east (verse 32) and finally to the north (verse 35). Here again measurements were taken and Ezekiel recorded all the details. Ezekiel took note of the rooms where they washed the burnt offerings (verse 38). He saw the tables where they laid the animals down to kill them and prepare them for sacrifice (verses 39–43). Built into the walls of the inner court were various chambers. These chambers were used for the singers and priests who were involved in the worship services (verses 44–46). There was also an altar in this inner court (verse 47).

In chapter 41 Ezekiel and the man with the measuring rod moved into the sanctuary of the temple. From the inner court of the temple, they had to ascend another flight of stairs to reach the sanctuary (40:49). The sanctuary itself was divided into two parts (verses 1–4). The outer room is labeled as "Holy Place" on our chart. The innermost room was the called the "Most Holy Place" by Ezekiel's guide and is labeled as the "Holy of Holies" on our chart. This inner chamber was where God's presence resided. Around the sanctuary was a series of rooms inset into the outer walls (verses 6–7). There were three floors of rooms with thirty rooms on each level, making ninety rooms in all (verse 6). The rooms measured four cubits in width (2 meters or 6 feet). Of particular interest to Ezekiel were the carvings of cherubim and palm trees on the sanctuary walls (verses 18–20).

In chapter 42, after seeing the temple, the man with the measuring rod took Ezekiel to the east gate of the inner court (verse 1). Here again Ezekiel noted the details of the three stories of rooms. As he examined these rooms, the man with the rod explained that some of these chambers served as places for the priests to eat the holy offerings (verse 13). Other spaces were used for the storage of grain and other holy offerings (verse 13).

In chapter 43 Ezekiel's guide brought him to the east gate of the temple (verse 1) Here Ezekiel heard a voice like rushing waters and saw the earth become radiant with the glory of the Lord (verse 2). Ezekiel fell down on his face at the sight of the glory of God (verse 3). This was not the first time that the prophet had had this experience. He reminds us in verse 3 that the vision he saw then was like the one he saw at the Kebar River in chapter 1. As he lay there on his face in this vision, the glory of the Lord came from the east and filled the temple. The Spirit of God lifted Ezekiel up to his feet and brought him into the inner court. The glory of God had filled that inner court. Here in the midst of this tremendous glory, Ezekiel heard the voice of God speaking to him. God told him that he would live in this temple in the presence of his people (verse 7). He promised that Israel would no longer defile his holy name. This voice reminded Ezekiel of the terrible abominations that his people had committed. Knowing what Ezekiel was thinking, God told him that it was now time to end all the rebellion of his people so they could return to him. God then commanded Ezekiel to share the plans of the temple with his people so that they would be ashamed and return to him (verse 10).

What does all this mean? What does it have to do with us today? It is possible that this prophecy was, in part, fulfilled when the people of God returned from exile and rebuilt the temple in Jerusalem. God gave them a picture of the temple to encourage and give hope to his people in exile. This picture showed his people that he had not forsaken them. The day would come when they would worship him again.

It is important to note here that Ezekiel 38–47 has many similarities to Revelation 20–22. Consider the following similarities:

- There is a description of Gog and Magog (Ezekiel 38–39; Revelation 20:7–10).
- After the destruction of Gog and Magog, there is a vision of a new city (Ezekiel 40–43; Revelation 21).
- In both passages the city is measured with a measuring rod (Ezekiel 40:5; Revelation 21:15).

- There is a river flowing out from the throne (Ezekiel 47:1; Revelation 22:1).
- The river flowing from the throne gives life to fruit trees bearing fruit each month. The leaves and the fruit of these trees have healing power (Ezekiel 47:12; Revelation 22:2).

Could this Ezekiel passage be the Old Testament equivalent to Revelation 20–22? Is the complete fulfilment of the prophecy of Ezekiel yet to be seen? If John is seeing the same temple, it is obvious that the fulfillment of the prophecy of Ezekiel had not yet taken place when John wrote.

While there is much speculation over the hidden meaning of this temple, there is a very practical lesson for us here in these chapters. What does God do for his people in these chapters? His people were in exile. Their minds were saturated with the problems they encountered on a daily basis because of their exile. They were tempted to become discouraged in their difficulties. God was reaching out to them. He set before them a very detailed plan of a temple. This plan was to be a great encouragement to his people. God promised them that the day was coming when they would be freed from their oppression. God challenged them to take their minds off their problems and focus on his promises.

Is it not in the difficult moments that we need to be reminded of what God has in store for us? There is nothing that will lift our spirits more than the reminder of the glories that await us. When we recall what God has promised to those who love him, our heavy hearts are lightened. Our discouragement melts away. Our fears are calmed. Hope is restored. Our spirits are lifted up into worship and adoration. When things are not going as you had hoped and you are tempted to be discouraged, take a look at the plans for the temple and be reassured. Let the promises of God renew your heart and lift your soul out of the depth of despair into worship and adoration.

For Consideration:

- What encouragement do you suppose the people of God would have received from this particular vision of Ezekiel?

- Are you going through a difficult trial right now? What personal application do you take from this section of Scripture?

- Make a list of some of the glories promised you in Scripture. How does this help you gain perspective in your trials?

For Prayer:

- Thank God for the glorious promises he offers you in his Word today.

- Take one of those promises and ask God to help you to face your problem with the assurance that he will be true to his Word.

- Ask God to set your heart upon his promises.

42

Separated Unto Him

Read Ezekiel 43:13–44:31

How important is the condition of our hearts in the worship and service of God? Can we allow his work to be done by men and women who are not serious about their personal walk with God? Can we say we have truly worshiped God if we have done so without dealing with our sins? In the Old Testament God took worship very seriously. His work was to be done by those whom he had particularly chosen. These people needed to be right with him. They could not take their task lightly. Nothing was to be done in a careless fashion. Both the priests and the articles of worship needed to be set apart for the Lord's exclusive use. In chapters 43 and 44 of Ezekiel, the prophet described God's laws regarding worship and service in his holy temple.

Altar (43:13–27)

We discover first of all that the articles of worship were to be set apart for the exclusive use of the Lord. We have in Ezekiel 43:13–27 a description of the law of God concerning the dedication of an altar. Let us look briefly at what God required.

Before the altar could be used, it needed to be dedicated to the Lord. The dedication of the altar took seven days (verse 25). On the first day a young bull was sacrificed (verse 19). To purify the altar, his blood was to be placed on the horns of the altar and around its rim (verse 20). The young bull was then burned outside the sanctuary (verse 21). On the second day of the dedication of the altar, a male goat was sacrificed as a sin offering. His blood also was sprinkled on the altar (verse 22). Also on that day a young bull and a ram were sacrificed as a burnt offering with salt (verse 23). For the remainder of the seven days, a male goat, a young bull, and a ram were sacrificed before the Lord (verse 25). Only after the altar had been purified for seven days in this manner would the Lord accept the offerings that were made on it. This procedure for dedicating the altar set it apart for the exclusive worship of God.

Sanctuary (44:1–3)

God took Ezekiel to the outer gate of the sanctuary. This gate was to remain shut (verse 2). The reason stated for this was "because the LORD, the God of Israel has entered through it." In the Old Testament context, the presence of the Lord was revealed particularly in the sanctuary of the temple. The ordinary Israelite was not permitted to be where God resided. Only the priests could approach for the purpose of ministering before the Lord.

We read in verse 3 that the prince was granted permission to come to the gate or threshold of the sanctuary where he was to worship the Lord. Ezekiel 46:1–2 adds further light here. The prince was to come with an offering for the people. He was to bring this offering to the gate where it would be given to the priests. The prince could worship at the threshold but was not permitted to enter the sanctuary itself.

As if to reaffirm the sanctity of the sanctuary, the Lord brought Ezekiel out into the outer court to the front of the temple. As Ezekiel looked back at the temple of God, he saw the glory of God filling it (verse 4). As he watched he fell on his face before the glory of God. It was indeed an awesome sight. It certainly confirmed in his mind the holiness and sanctity of the temple.

Temple Ministries (44:6–9)

In Ezekiel 44:6–9 God confronted his people with one of their detestable practices. It seems that they had been bringing "the uncircumcised in heart" into the temple and allowing them to be involved in the ministries of the temple (verses 8–9). In Numbers 18:4 God commanded that the temple duties be performed by the Levites and the priests only. Could it be that these priests felt that they were above some of these menial tasks? God reminded them that even the lowliest duties were to be performed by qualified individuals. They were profaning his name by giving these duties to foreigners. Are we not guilty of this practice in our churches today? Who is involved in the various ministries of your church today? Do you have choir members or Sunday School teachers who are living in sin? Do the greeters and ushers know the Lord Jesus as their personal Lord and Savior? Are those who sing the special music in your church walking with the Lord? God is telling us here that it is of utmost importance that those who serve him in public ministry be in a right relationship with him. Could it be that the blessing of God is withheld from our ministries because those who perform these ministries are not right with God?

Priests (44:10–31)

God then spoke concerning the priests. These individuals also needed to be separated particularly unto the Lord. It seems that some Levites had wandered away from the Lord and were serving idols (verse 10). While they were bowing down to these idols, they were also serving in the temple (verse 11). God saw their hypocrisy. He knew their hearts. He was not pleased with them. In recent years we have heard horror stories about what happens behind the closed doors of our churches. The servant of God was to be without hypocrisy. He was to serve with clean hands and a pure heart. God was against these leaders who lived a lie. They were not to come near him to serve. They would bear the shame and the guilt of their evil ways (verse 13). Instead, they were to be restricted to the servile duties of the temple (verse 14). They were not to touch the holy articles used in the worship of God. They were barred from approaching the Lord as priests. They were found to be unworthy of the service of the Lord. Only those who had remained faithful to the Lord and had not bowed the knee to idols could stand before him and minister. Only these priests could enter the temple (verse 16). God shows us that the only people fit to serve him are those who have turned their backs upon sin. God's ministers are to be separated unto him. They must live pure lives.

Priestly Garments (44:16–19)

In regard to the clothing of the priests, they were to be made of linen. The priest was to wear nothing that would cause him to perspire, as this would make his offering unclean (verse 18). When he was finished performing his duties, the priest was to remove his priestly garments and leave them within the temple. These garments were not to be taken from the temple area. Even the garments of the priest were separated unto God. They needed to be kept pure and clean for the worship of the Lord alone.

Lifestyle of the Priest (44:20–27)

Priests were to live a special life of separation unto the Lord. They were neither to shave their heads nor grow long hair. They had to have their hair well-trimmed at all times (verse 20). They were forbidden to drink wine when they entered into the inner court of the temple (verse 21). Priests were only to marry virgins or the widow of another priest. They could not marry a divorced woman (verse 22). They were to be careful to teach Israel the difference between clean and unclean things. They were to instruct Israel in the difference between what was holy and what was common (verse 23). They were to judge cases according to the holy Word of God (verse 24). A priest was not to defile himself by touching a dead body unless it was a close relative (verse 25). If he had to touch a dead body, he would be required to go through seven days of purification. During this time, he needed to offer a sin offering to the Lord before he could go back to his duties as a priest (verses 26–27). While they were to have no land, they were to be given its best products for food (verses 28–30). They were to be careful about what they ate. They could eat nothing that would render them unclean (verse 31).

What does all of this teach us? Does it not remind us that God's servants must be separated unto him? God's servants must be holy men and women. Our sins will render our services unclean. God is not only concerned about getting the job done; he is also concerned about how the job gets done. Our hearts and our lives must be pure if we want to serve the Lord. Does this passage not call us to carefully examine our lives? Are we living up to the standards that God has set out for us? Are we men and women of sincerity? Do we practice what we preach?

Are you a Sunday School teacher? Is your life an example for your children? Are you an elder or deacon in a local church? Do you live up to the standards you preach to others? In our day, more than ever before, we need men and women fully consecrated to God. Our society has heard us preach, but have they seen us live the message we preach? Our age has seen the fall of many evangelists and Christian workers. People have seen the hypocrisy that goes on behind the scenes. God is calling us through this passage to re-examine ourselves in light of his Word. Where are the men and women who are set apart entirely for the glory of God? Where are the men and women of our day who will turn aside from the polluting influences of our modern age and consecrate themselves fully to God? God expects that we, his servants, be completely separated unto him.

For Consideration:

• Are we guilty of the practices of Israel here in this chapter? In what ways have we not separated ourselves unto the Lord?

• Are there areas in your life that would hinder you from service to the Lord?

• Why is it so tempting to populate our ministries and churches with unbelieving or disobedient Christians? Is it wrong to have unbelievers in your church? What is the difference between evangelizing the lost and using the lost to minister in Christ's name?

For Prayer:

• Ask God to search your heart to see if there is anything that you need to confess before going out to minister in his name.

• Ask God to help you to see if there is any way that you have shown disrespect for his work by your actions or attitudes.

• Thank God that he is a holy God but still willing to reach out to us as sinners.

43

The Prince of Israel

Read Ezekiel 45–46

I n Ezekiel 40–43 God gave his people the promise of a
new temple. Ezekiel 43 and 44 spoke about the priests
and the worship in this new temple. Chapters 45 and 46
spelled out the responsibilities of the prince or the political
leader of Israel.

Chapter 45 begins by telling us that when the people
of God "divide the land by lot into inheritance" (verse 1
NKJV), they were to set aside a portion of land for the Lord
as a sacred district around the new temple. I have included a
diagram to help us to understand verses 1–8.

This sacred district (about 8 miles by 3 miles) was to be
divided into four main sections. The first portion of land was
set apart for the temple and the use of the priests who served
the Lord in the temple. On this piece of land the priests could
build their homes (verses 2–4). By this means they could
live close to their work. The second piece of land was given
to the other Levites (verse 5). On this land they could build

Figure 43.1

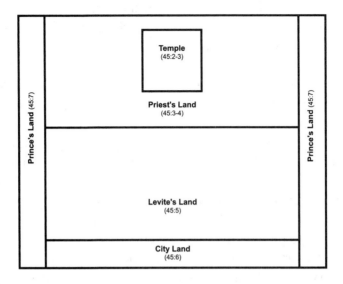

communities to live in. The actual size of this land was the same as the land given to the priests. The third division of land was smaller than the others and was given as common land to the city (Jerusalem). It was for the use of the common people (verse 6). This land could be used for houses and pastureland (48:15). Along the sides of these three portions of land were the sections allotted to the prince of the land of Israel (verse 7). This was the general allotment of the sacred district of land that was to be set aside to the Lord around the temple.

Having explained to his people the allotment of the land, God then focused his attention on the princes or political rulers of the land. They were the ones who would govern the secular affairs of the nation. God had some important things to say to anyone ruling his people.

He was to be content with his land allotment

First, the prince was to be content with the land the Lord had allotted to him and his family (45:8). He was not to oppress the people because he had a portion that was sufficient for his needs. While it was possible for the prince to offer some of his land as a gift to his servants, the land would revert automatically back to the prince in the year of Jubilee (46:16–17). In other words, the land could not be given away forever. This would discourage any future princes from taking land that was not theirs. God reminded the prince that he was not to take away the inheritance of his servants (46:18). He was not to seek more than his share of land at the expense of others. The prince already had all the land he needed. He was not to allow his greed to accumulate any more than the Lord had given to him. The prince was to be a servant of his people. He was not to use his power to increase his own wealth and prosperity. He was not to use violence to plunder his people (verse 9). He was not to take away the land God had given to his people by dispossessing them (verse 9). God knew that the lust for power and riches would be very real. That same temptation exists today.

The prince was to be a person of integrity (45:9–16)

Second, the prince was to be a man of integrity. In verses 9–12 the Lord reviewed the weights and measurements used in Israel. His scales were to be accurate. He was to deal honestly with his people. He was not to take any more then was rightfully his. God also spelled out for his people just what he required them to give to the prince (verses 13–16). The people were to set aside one-sixtieth of their grain and one percent of their oil. One sheep out of every two hundred belonged to the prince (verse 15). By specifying what he required of his people, God encouraged honesty and fair dealing on the part of the prince.

The prince was to be generous

Third, the prince was to provide for the needs of his people. Out of the resources that were given to him, the prince was to offer up grain offerings, burnt offerings, and drink offerings for the people (45:17). God spelled out for the prince his responsibilities concerning sacrifices and offerings to the LORD. On the first day of the first month (the New Year), the prince was to bring a young bull without blemish to the sanctuary for the annual purification of the temple (45: 18). The blood of this bull was placed on the doorposts, on the altar, and on the gateposts of the inner court. On the fourteenth day of the first month (Passover), the prince was to provide— every day for seven days—seven bulls, seven rams, and one goat for sacrifice. He was also to provide the agreed amount of grain and oil for these daily sacrifices (45:24). Every Sabbath the prince of the people was to come to the temple of the Lord. He was to bring with him six male lambs, one ram, and the agreed amount of grain and oil for the sacrifices (46:4–5). For the special celebration of the New Moon, the prince added a young bull to the weekly Sabbath offering (46: 6–7). Every day the prince was required to offer "to the LORD" a one-year-old lamb and the agreed amount of grain and oil offerings (46:13–15). From time to time the prince could also offer a free will offering for the people (46:11–12). These offerings could not be taken lightly. The prince of Israel had to be faithful to God in bringing his sacrifices daily to the temple for the people. In all this he was to spend of his own resources to facilitate the worship of the God of Israel.

The prince was to worship the LORD God
    Fourth, the prince was to be with the people in their worship (46:10). He was not to shirk from his own responsibility to be in the assembly of God to worship with the people. He was to be an example to his people in the worship of God. If he was to lead God's people, he was to be in a right relationship with God himself.
    In the remaining verses of chapter 46, the man who was showing Ezekiel the temple showed him where these offerings were to be prepared. In the corners of the outer

court were ledges of stone with a fireplace beneath. It was in these areas that the sacrifices and offerings which the prince brought to the temple were prepared (see 46:19–24).

We have already seen that God required that his people and the articles used in his worship be set apart wholly for himself. In this city where the temple was (Jerusalem), God required that the princes of the people be men who were content with what they had (they were not greedy for gain). They were to deal with people in all honesty (they were to take only what was required). They were to be generous men who led their people by example in worship of God.

What would our nation be like if our political leaders illustrated these characteristics in their lives? What a different place our country would be if our political leaders took seriously Ezekiel 45 and 46. How we need to see in our day men and women in leadership who are content with what they have, honest and generous in their dealings, and who humbly bow the knee before God! May God give us men and women like this in our government today.

For Consideration:

- How do the leaders of our day measure up to the standards God laid out for his princes here in this chapter?

- What does this chapter indicate to us about the temptations that those in leadership face today?

For Prayer:

- Take a moment to pray for your political leaders. Ask God to help them be the people God wants them to be.

44

The River Of Life and the New Jerusalem

Read Ezekiel 47–48

As his tour of the temple and the new city came to an end, Ezekiel was brought to the entrance of the temple. Here he saw a stream of water coming from under the eastern threshold (verse 1). This was not uncommon. Water was used in the temple to flush away the blood that was spilled in the sacrifice of many animals.

From here the prophet was taken outside the main gate that faced east. Ezekiel and his guide followed the stream as it wound its way to the east. Ezekiel's guide measured one thousand cubits (1500 feet or 450 meters), and the prophet noted that the water level had risen to his ankles (verse 3). One thousand cubits more were measured, and the water level had risen to his knees (verse 4). As they traveled yet another one thousand cubits, the level rose to the prophet's waist (verse 4). By the time they had traveled one thousand cubits more, the stream had become a great river that could not be crossed (verse 5).

At this point Ezekiel's guide brought him to the bank of the river. On each side of the river, the prophet could see many trees (verse 7). They were fed by the river flowing out of the sanctuary. They produced fruit every month. Their fruit was for nourishment and healing (verse 12). It is important here that we compare what Ezekiel saw with what the apostle John saw in his vision in Revelation. The apostle John recorded in Revelation 22 that he saw a similar river. It too flowed from the throne of God. On each side of John's river grew the tree of life producing twelve crops of fruit each year. The leaves of this tree were used for the healing of the nations (Revelation 22:1–2). Did these two men share the same vision?

As this river flowed eastward, it went through a valley (verse 8). Wherever it went, it brought prosperity and new life (verse 9). When it emptied itself into the sea, it healed the sea of its impurities (verse 8). The image here was of a sea that was so salty that it could not sustain life. However, when the river emptied itself into the sea, the waters were healed so they could sustain life. The result was a sea that produced a great multitude of fish of all kinds (verse 9). The fishermen were pictured here standing by the shores of this great sea hauling in an abundance of fish of all kinds (verse 10). We learn in verse 11 that there were certain swamps and marshes that were not healed but were given over to salt.

What does all this mean? It seems that God was telling Ezekiel that many blessings would flow from the temple of God to the world. The river of God's blessing would flow through the valleys and deserts, bringing blessing and healing wherever it went. It would flow into basins of evil and sin and bring new life and vitality. The amazing thing about this river is how it seemed to gain momentum and become larger and deeper as it flowed. More and more people were being caught up in this river of God's blessing.

Notice, however, that this river did not heal all places. There remained certain swamplands that would continue to be untouched (verse 11). There will always be those who are resistant to the movement of God's Spirit. It should be noticed here that, unlike the desert, the marshes and swamps sustained life. Here in these marshes there was water and food. There are many churches and ministries like this. They have a certain life in themselves. They attract people because of their doctrinal positions or friendly atmosphere. They are resistant, however, to the greater work of God's Spirit. In the history of revivals, there have always been those who refused to accept what God was doing. Notice here that these swamps and marshes were eventually given over to salt (verse 11). The life they did have would be taken from them and they would perish.

In verses 13–23 God explained to the prophet the boundaries of the land he would give to his people. The land was to be divided among his people by tribe. What is important to note here is the fact that the foreigner who lived with them was also to be considered as a native Israelite (verse 22). In whatever tribe they lived, they were considered part of that tribe and received an inheritance as a full Israelite with the others. God had always told his people that they were to respect the strangers that were among them: "The alien living with you must be treated as one of your native-born. Love him as yourself, for you were aliens in Egypt. I am the LORD your God" (Leviticus 19:34). "You are to have the same law for the alien and the native-born. I am the LORD your God" (Leviticus 24:22).

The fact that these strangers were receiving an inheritance as full children of God shows us that the door was wide open for the foreigner to become a child of God. This great river of God's blessing flowing from the temple would span the globe and draw in the Gentile nations. Those who believe in the Lord today have been drawn into this great family of God.

In Ezekiel 48, verses 1–7 and 24–29 described the division of the land of Israel among the twelve tribes. Verses 9–28 focused once again on the piece of land that was to be given over to the LORD. We have already described the division of this sacred district in the last chapter. Verses 9–12 focus on the section of land given over to the priests (see diagram in the last chapter). The temple was to be in the center of this parcel of land. The priests who had remained faithful to the Lord and had not bowed the knee to idols were to live and work on this parcel of land (verse 11). The detailed measurements for the land given to the other priests can be found in verses 13–15. Here these priests could buy and sell property (verse 14).

The city was to be built on the third portion of land. The detail of this parcel of land is described for us in verses 15–19. The prince's land was located on both sides of the land given to the priests and city. The description of this land is in verse 21. In verses 22–29 we have the allotment of land to the various tribes of Israel.

This chapter is closed with a short description of the wall that surrounded the city itself. The wall of the city would have twelve gates. Each of the gates would be named after one of the tribes of Israel. There were to be three gates on the north side of the city named after Reuben, Judah, and Levi (verse 31). The three gates on the east side of the city were named after the tribes of Joseph (Ephraim and Manasseh combined; see Genesis 48:5, 6, 22), Benjamin, and Dan (verse 32). The gates of Simeon, Issachar, and Zebulun were located on the south side of the city (verse 33). The remaining three gates of Gad, Asher, and Naphtali were located on the west (verse 34).

In our comparison of Ezekiel's vision with that of the apostle John, it is important to note that the city that John saw also had twelve gates named after the twelve tribes of Israel: "It had a great, high wall with twelve gates, and with twelve angels at the gates. On the gates were written the names of the twelve tribes of Israel. There were three gates on the east, three on the north, three on the south and three on the west" (Revelation 21:12–13).

History has not yet seen the fulfillment of Ezekiel's prophecy.[1] The temple and the city he saw are yet to be revealed. While John and Ezekiel had similar visions, there are some important differences. Ezekiel saw a temple in the city of his vision. On the other hand, John tells us in Revelation 21:22 that there was no temple in the New Jerusalem, for the Lamb himself was its temple. In Ezekiel's vision of the temple, the Levitical priests offered sacrifices to the Lord for the sins of the people (see Ezekiel 46:19–24). These sacrifices would no longer be necessary in the New Jerusalem. The death of the Lord Jesus put an end to the sacrificial system of the Old Testament. Since history has not revealed this temple and the city to us, we have one of two choices to make. Either we interpret Ezekiel's vision symbolically or we take it literally. It would seem to me that if we take John's vision of the New Jerusalem literally, we should also treat Ezekiel's vision in the same way. The clear reference to the Jewish sacrificial system would lead us to believe that Ezekiel was referring to the Jewish nation here. Scripture tells us that the day is coming when the Lord will again draw his people to himself (see Romans 11:25–26). Paul asked his readers in Romans 11:12 that if the Jewish rejection of Christ meant the salvation of countless Gentiles, what would their acceptance of Christ bring? From Ezekiel's temple the blessing of God flowed. We may yet be surprised at the wonderful work that God will do through the Jewish nation in the days to come.

What a hope is ours today if we know the Lord Jesus as our personal Savior! The day is coming when you and I will travel to that city to dwell in the presence of the Lord. I remind you, however, that not just anyone will be granted entrance to this great city. Revelation 21:27 tells us: "Nothing impure will ever enter it, nor will anyone who does what is shameful or deceitful, but only those whose names are written in the Lamb's book of life."

Yes, only those whose names are written in the Lamb's book of life will be granted entrance. Are you sure that when you approach the gates of the city and they search for your name in the book of life that your name will be there? If you are not sure, today is the day to cry out to God. He alone can write your name in this registry. Won't you cry out to him right now?

From Ezekiel's temple would flow a great river. That river would span the globe and bring blessing and renewal and healing wherever it went. Those who had tasted of the river of life would populate that new city. Have you experienced the blessings of this river?

For Consideration:

• What evidence is there of the blessings of Ezekiel's river today?

• What keeps people today from yielding to the ministry of God's Spirit?

• Have you been healed and renewed by Ezekiel's river?

For Prayer:

• Ask God to pour out this river of blessing on you today.

• Ask him to reveal any obstacles that stand in the way of his abundant blessing in your life or the life of your church.

Endnotes

Chapter 29
1. Some commentaries state that a possible interpretation held by some believers is that verses 12–19 may also be referring to Satan, the supernatural evil power behind the King of Tyre. See Matthew Henry, *Matthew Henry's Commentary on the Whole Bible*, vol 4, (Peabody, MA: Hendrickson Publishers, 1992), pp. 721–722. See also Adam Clarke, "Job-Malachi," in *Clarke's Commentary* (Nashville: Abingdon, no date), p. 500, comment on verse 15.

Chapter 41
1. One particular literal view held by some believers is that Ezekiel 40–48 describes the conditions when Christ comes to rule on earth for 1000 years. This section includes the millennial temple (40:1–43:12), millennial worship (43:13–46:24), and the millennial apportionment of the land (47:1–48:35). See J.D. Douglas and Merrill C. Tenney, eds., "Temple," in *The New International Dictionary of the Bible* (Grand Rapids: Zondervan, 1987), p. 993. See also John MacArthur, *The MacArthur Study Bible* (Nashville: Word, 1997), p. 1290, comment on Ezekiel 40:1.

Chapter 44
1. See endnote 1 on chapter 41.

Light To My Path
Devotional Commentary Series

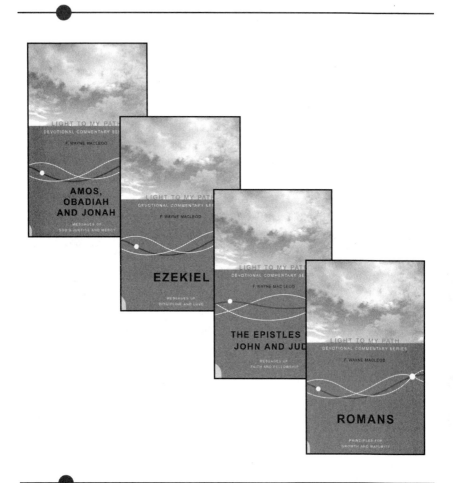

Now Available

Old Testament
- Ezekiel
- Amos, Obadiah, and Jonah

New Testament
- Romans
- The Epistles of John and Jude

A new commentary series for every day devotional use.

- Messages of Discipline and Love

- Messages of God's Justice and Mercy

- Principles for Growth and Maturity

- Messages of Faith and Fellowship

Watch for more in the series
available Fall 2004

Old Testament
- Ezra, Nehemiah, and Esther
- Micah, Nahum, Habakkuk, and Zephaniah

New Testament
- John
- Acts

Other books available from Authentic Media . . .

Authentic
MEDIA

PO Box 1047
129 Mobilization Drive
Waynesboro, GA 30830

706-554-1594
1-8MORE-BOOKS
authenticusa@stl.org

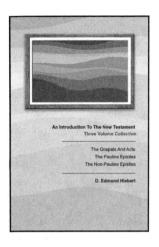

An Introduction To The New Testament
Three Volume Collection

D. Edmond Hiebert

Though not a commentary, the Introduction to the New Testament presents each book's message along with a discussion of such questions as authorship, composition, historical circumstances of their writing, issues of criticism and provides helpful, general information on their content and nature. The bibliographies and annotated book list are extremely helpful for pastors, teachers, and laymen as an excellent invitation to further careful exploration.

This book will be prized by all who have a desire to delve deeply into the New Testament writings.

Volume 1: The Gospels And Acts
Volume 2: The Pauline Epistles
Volume 3: The Non-Pauline Epistles and Revelation

1-884543-74-X   976 Pages

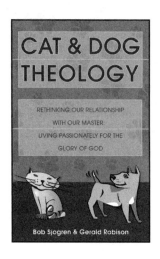

Cat and Dog Theology
Rethinking Our Relationship With Our Master

Bob Sjogren & Dr. Gerald Robison

There is a joke about cats and dogs that conveys their differences perfectly.

> A dog says, "You pet me, you feed me, you shelter me, you love me, you must be God."
>
> A cat says, "You pet me, you feed me, you shelter me, you love me, I must be God."

These God-given traits of cats ("You exist to serve me") and dogs ("I exist to serve you") are often similar to the theological attitudes we have in our view of God and our relationship to Him. Using the differences between cats and dogs in a light-handed manner, the authors compel us to challenge our thinking in deep and profound ways. As you are drawn toward God and the desire to reflect His glory in your life, you will worship, view missions, and pray in a whole new way. This life-changing book will give you a new perspective and vision for God as you delight in the God who delights in you.

1-884543-17-0   206 Pages